USSR
(UNION OF SOVIET SOCIALIST REPUBLICS)

Associated Press
Wednesday 31 July:

Signs of Soviet and Warsaw Pact mobilisation and movement towards the Iron Curtain has the leaders of NATO concerned, prompting the French President to confirm France's commitment to NATO and the defence of Western Europe from outside aggression. This comes on the heels of the US President's order federalizing Army Reserve and National Guards for service overseas on 28 July. Many US troops are already reporting for duty and preparing for deployment.

CNN Report
Saturday 3 August:

"I'm standing here in the West German border town of Hof, passing by are the tanks and armoured personnel carriers of the 2nd Cavalry Regiment, the 7th Corps unit responsible for security along the frontier in this sector. With me is Captain Jeff Haines, what can you tell be of the situation?"

"Well Sir, there is an increased level of activity by the East German and Soviet forces along the border area."

"Have there been incidents?"

"No, so far they have kept to their side of the border."

ABC News Report
Wednesday 7 August:

"I'm standing here outside the gates of Fort Bragg as the last of the trucks full of soldiers from the 82nd Airborne Division leave for parts unknown. Since the Warsaw Pack crossed the inner German border three days ago, speculation has been rife as to whether the Ready Reaction Force would be committed to the war in Europe or held for operations elsewhere. It seems they have been committed, but where?"

New York Times
Thursday 8 August:

Fighting in southern Germany has been raging for four days and the divisions of the US 7th Corps have been fighting a dogged defense against the armored spearheads of the Soviet and Czechoslovakian armies. On 7 August the 1st 'Old Ironsides' Armored Division was finally forced to fall back from Bayreuth towards Nürnberg, where they once again established strong lines of defense. The 1st and 3rd Infantry Divisions further strengthened the defense, holding the Warsaw Pact thrusts at every turn.

CNN Delayed Report
Thursday 15 August:

"I'm here aboard the USS Saipan as we sail the North Sea to the Jutland Peninsula where the 2nd Marine Division, and other elements of the 2nd Marine Amphibious Force, will soon be making an amphibious landing to reinforce NATO forces in Denmark. With me now is Gunnery Sergeant Malcolm Wheatley. Are the men ready for what might await them?"

"Yes Ma'am, Marines are prepared for every eventuality and we will not turn from any challenge or adversity ahead of us."

BLACK SEA

TURKEY

IRAN

SYRIA

IRAQ

KUWAIT

STRAIT OF HORMUZ

LEBANON

PERSIAN GULF

NEAN

JORDAN

SAUDI ARABIA

ISRAEL

UAE

EGYPT

IT'S 1985 AND THE COLD WAR JUST GOT HOT!

Team Yankee is a complete set of rules for playing World War III Wargames.

Based on the book written by Harold Coyle in 1987, Team Yankee brings the conflict that simmered throughout the Cold War to life. You will command your troops in miniature on a realistic battlefield.

In Team Yankee, a heavy combat team of M1 Abrams tanks and M113 armoured personnel carriers faces a Soviet invasion of West Germany. Outnumbered and outgunned, Captain Sean Bannon and his men will have to fight hard and they'll have to fight smart if they are going to survive.

Lt. Colonel Yuri Potecknov's motor rifle battalion is preparing to execute its mission in the scientific manner that he had been taught at the Frunze Military Academy and used in Afghanistan. Victory today will bring the world proletarian revolution that much closer.

Find out more at:

WWW.TEAM-YANKEE.COM

© Copyright Battlefront Miniatures Ltd., 2017. ISBN: 9780994147455

STRIPES

US FORCES IN WORLD WAR III

Written by: Wayne Turner and Phil Yates
Editors: Peter Simunovich, John-Paul Brisigotti
Graphic Design: Casey Davies,
Assistant Graphic Design: Sean Goodison, Morgan Cannon
Miniatures Design: Evan Allen, Tim Adcock, Matt Bickley, Will Jayne
Cover Art and Illustrations: Vincent Wai
Miniatures Painting: Aaron Mathie
Stories by: Nigel Slater
Web Support: Charlie Roberts, Chris Townley

Proof Readers: David Adlam, Tom Culpepper, Mark Goddard,
Alan Graham, Sean Ireland, Henry Johnson, Luke Parsonage,
Ben Polikoff, Duncan Stradling, Stephen Smith, Garry Wait
Playtest Groups: Dad's Army (Gavin Van Rossum),
Historical Tabletop Gaming Society (Shane Kua),
Kampfgruppe Wilmington (Hunter Lanier),
Northern Battle Gamers (Nigel Slater),
The Rat Patrol (Kevin Hovanec),
The Yanks (Mitchell Landrum).

CONTENTS

NATO AND WARSAW PACT DEPLOYMENT AND PLANNED WARSAW PACT ATTACKS

Kiel

Rostock

Wilhelmshaven

Bremerhaven

Hamburg

Lübeck

LANDJUT
xxxx
NORTHAG

1ST NETHERLANDS CORPS

Bremen

2
GUA
TA
AR

xxx

1ST GERMAN CORPS

THE NETHERLANDS

xxx

1ST BRITISH CORPS

Hannover

3RD US CORPS

3RD SHOCK ARMY

Magdeburg

xxx

1ST BELGIUM CORPS

EA

3RD FRENCH CORPS

Essen

GROUP C
SOVIET FOR
IN GERMA
(GSFG)

Düsseldorf

NORTHAG
xxxx
CENTAG

Cologne

3RD GERMAN CORPS

Leipzig

BONN

8TH GUARDS ARMY

xxx

WEST GERMANY

Fulda

5TH US CORPS

Frankfurt

xxx

Rhine River

7TH US CORPS

Saarbrücken

Nürnberg

CENTAG
xxxx
SOUTHAG

FRANCE

1ST FRENCH CORPS

Stuttgart

2ND GERMAN CORPS

2ND FRENCH CORPS

Danube River

Munich

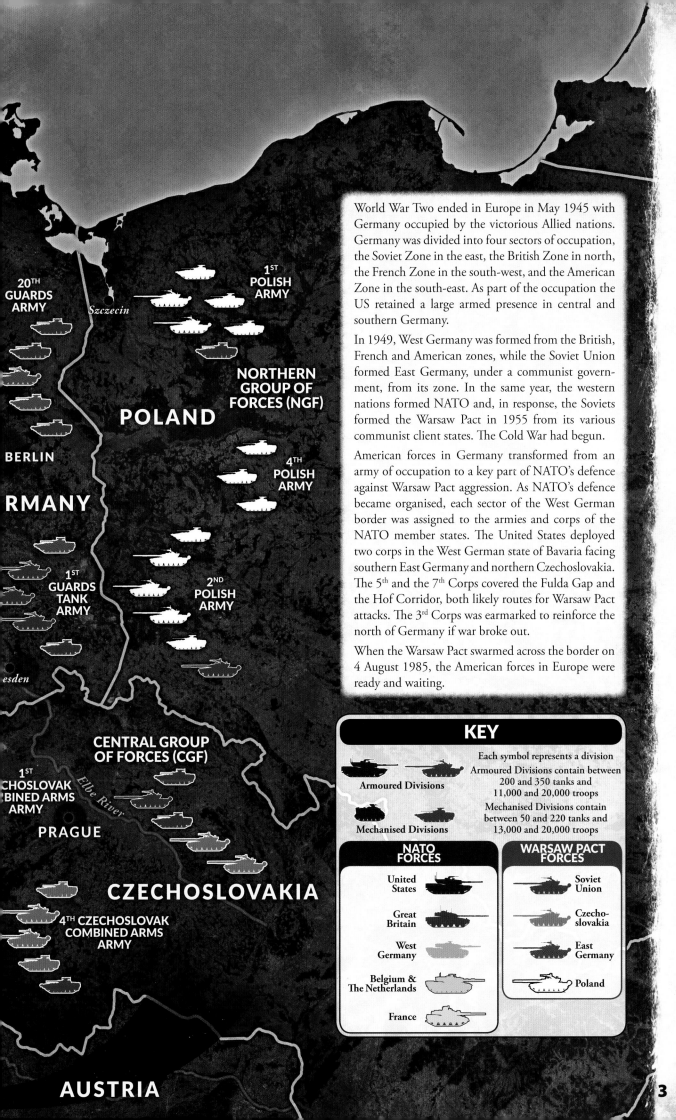

20TH GUARDS ARMY

Szczecin

1ST POLISH ARMY

NORTHERN GROUP OF FORCES (NGF)

POLAND

BERLIN

RMANY

4TH POLISH ARMY

1ST GUARDS TANK ARMY

2ND POLISH ARMY

esden

CENTRAL GROUP OF FORCES (CGF)

1ST CHOSLOVAK BINED ARMS ARMY

Elbe River

PRAGUE

CZECHOSLOVAKIA

4TH CZECHOSLOVAK COMBINED ARMS ARMY

AUSTRIA

World War Two ended in Europe in May 1945 with Germany occupied by the victorious Allied nations. Germany was divided into four sectors of occupation, the Soviet Zone in the east, the British Zone in north, the French Zone in the south-west, and the American Zone in the south-east. As part of the occupation the US retained a large armed presence in central and southern Germany.

In 1949, West Germany was formed from the British, French and American zones, while the Soviet Union formed East Germany, under a communist govern-ment, from its zone. In the same year, the western nations formed NATO and, in response, the Soviets formed the Warsaw Pact in 1955 from its various communist client states. The Cold War had begun.

American forces in Germany transformed from an army of occupation to a key part of NATO's defence against Warsaw Pact aggression. As NATO's defence became organised, each sector of the West German border was assigned to the armies and corps of the NATO member states. The United States deployed two corps in the West German state of Bavaria facing southern East Germany and northern Czechoslovakia. The 5th and the 7th Corps covered the Fulda Gap and the Hof Corridor, both likely routes for Warsaw Pact attacks. The 3rd Corps was earmarked to reinforce the north of Germany if war broke out.

When the Warsaw Pact swarmed across the border on 4 August 1985, the American forces in Europe were ready and waiting.

KEY

Armoured Divisions

Each symbol represents a division

Armoured Divisions contain between 200 and 350 tanks and 11,000 and 20,000 troops

Mechanised Divisions

Mechanised Divisions contain between 50 and 220 tanks and 13,000 and 20,000 troops

NATO FORCES

United States	
Great Britain	
West Germany	
Belgium & The Netherlands	
France	

WARSAW PACT FORCES

Soviet Union	
Czecho-slovakia	
East Germany	
Poland	

US FORCES

The US 7th Corps is responsible for defending a sector of West Germany that straddles both the East German and Czechoslovakian Borders. Within this sector, stretching from Bad Kissingen in the north to Cham in the south, are a number of likely corridors for Warsaw Pact attacks.

The Hof Corridor consists of a break in the hilly terrain along the East German Border coupled with an extensive road network, making it a prime avenue of attack for the Soviet 1st Guards Tank Army stationed around Dresden. The Hof Corridor leads into Bavaria and onwards towards the Nurnberg and Stuttgart areas. The terrain is hilly, but contains a good road network for the breakout and exploitation once the narrow passes are breached.

The Soviet Central Group of Forces in Czechoslovakia and the Czechoslovakian 11th Combined Army also pose a threat from Cheb either south through Waldsassen or westwards through Schirnding where river valleys and plentiful roads also provide access through the hilly terrain leading down to the Danube Plain of Southern Bavaria and eventually Munich.

Watching the border and ready as the first line of defence is the 2nd Armored Cavalry Regiment operating from various camps near the border. If attacked, they fight delaying actions, holding the enemy for as long as possible, buying time for corps' reserves to deploy into position.

Behind the cavalry screen are the 3rd 'Rock of the Marne' Infantry Division (Mechanized) and the 1st 'Old Ironsides' Armored Division. These provide the core of the defence, powerful divisions capable of delivering the massive firepower required to stop a Soviet armoured assault.

In reserve is the 1st 'Big Red One' Infantry Division with its forward deployed equipment ready to be taken up by the division's personnel. They will fly in from their barracks in the United States, as practiced during regular Operation Reforger (Return of Forces to Germany) exercises. National Guards units, as well as ready reaction forces like the 82nd 'All American' Airborne Division can also be deployed in support.

TENSION BUILDS

As political tensions intensified over June and July 1985, US forces stepped up their readiness. The Reforger units had all their personnel put on alert and were ready for deployment to Germany once the orders were given. The US President issued an order federalizing the Army Reserve and National Guard on 28 July, allowing these troops to serve abroad. Meanwhile, regular troops stationed in West German had all leave cancelled and began preparations to mobilise, and in early July Reforger units began deploying from the United States to Germany. On 1 August NATO gave the order to mobilise all forces in preparation for war.

THE SOVIETS ATTACK

All through the day of 3 August reports streamed into the headquarters of the US 7th Corps detailing the increased activity of East German and Czechoslovakian troops along the border. 2nd Armored Cavalry Regiment and West German border guard watch posts had noticed increased patrolling, mine clearing, and generally a larger presence of troops. Radio, radar, satellite, and observation intelligence gave the 7th Corps commander a detailed picture of the Warsaw Pact activity on the border. It was clear that both the Hof Corridor and border areas near Cheb, Czechoslovakia could be potential avenues for attack.

In the early hours of 4 August, Soviet, East German, and Czechoslovakian forces began crossing the border in the 7th Corps sector. As predicted, cavalry posts were soon reporting forces crossings towards Hof from East Germany, as well as from Cheb in Czechoslovakia.

The corps' covering force, the 2nd Armored Cavalry Regiment, was first to see action. Their M1 Abrams tanks, M901 ITV missile carriers, and Cobra gunships meant the Warsaw Pact's initial push would be no easy task.

Around Hof the US cavalry was able to take advantage of ample hills, woods and small villages to ambush the Soviet forces of the 1st Guards Tank Army at every turn. The cavalry inflicted enough damage to divert or temporarily halt

each Soviet thrust, before withdrawing to a new position to do it again. Soviet and Czech forces advancing from Cheb found the conditions no different.

Throughout the morning of 4 August, the 2nd Armored Cavalry Regiment fought dogged delaying actions, only giving ground a little at a time. By mid-day the cavalry units around Hof had fought delaying actions through Münchberg to the passes leading to Bayreuth. There, they were bolstered by units from the 1st 'Old Ironsides' Armored Division. Further south from Cheb, Soviet forces had pushed directly westwards through Marktredwitz towards Bayreuth, while Czech forces pushed southwest towards Weiden.

Through the afternoon the Soviets threw units against the 1st Armored Division and 2nd Armored Cavalry forces holding the passes through the hills east of Bayreuth. Artillery, air strikes, infantry and armoured assaults all rained down on the US hill positions.

WORLD WAR III

Fighting lasted into the night, but by the close of 4 August Soviet forces had been unable to break the strong ring of defence around Bayreuth.

The 1st Armored Division's positions in front of Bayreuth held until 7 August when the Corps commander ordered them to withdraw southwest towards Erlangen and Nürnberg where they again took up defensive positions along hills to the east of the cities, defending the vital passes. Meanwhile, a brigade of the 3rd 'Rock of Marne' Infantry Division had taken up positions in the hills east of Bamberg, overlooking the city and the Regnitz and Main rivers. The 1st 'Big Red One' Infantry Division, having retrieved its POMCUS (Prepositioning Of Materiel Configured in Unit Sets) equipment from depots around Mannheim, had deployed around Ansbach, west of Nürnberg, ready to support both the 3rd Infantry and 1st Armored.

On 8 August, further hard fighting was seen along the line running through Bamberg, Erlangen, Nürnberg, and Ingolstadt (in the sector of the West German 2. Korps). Defensive ambushes and local counterattacks all along the 7th Corps front brought the Soviet and Czech advances to a halt. Czech units entered Nürnberg in the evening, which developed into savage close quarters fighting with elements of the 1st Armored Division. The battle lasted throughout the evening before the Czechs were pushed out though the town of Feucht and the surrounding woodland to the south of the city in the early hours of 9 August.

To the north 3rd Infantry Division forces launched ambushes as Soviet columns advanced from Bamberg near the town of Walsdorf.

The 3rd Infantry Division continued its fighting withdrawal to the Main River,

east of the city of Würzburg, where they finally brought the Soviet advance to a halt on 11 August.

To the south the 1st Armored Division had been pushed back towards Bad Windsheim and Ansbach after two divisions of the Czech 1st Combined Army had launched another vigorous assault on Nürnberg. However, by 10 August the Czech forward momentum had petered out as they ran into counterattacking forces from the 1st Infantry Division.

French forces had begun to arrive in the sector and began to take over the defensive positions of the US 7th Corps, freeing the corps to begin moving to the rear to prepare to take part in a counteroffensive towards the East German border. The fresh French divisions began to slowly grind back the Czechs and Soviets.

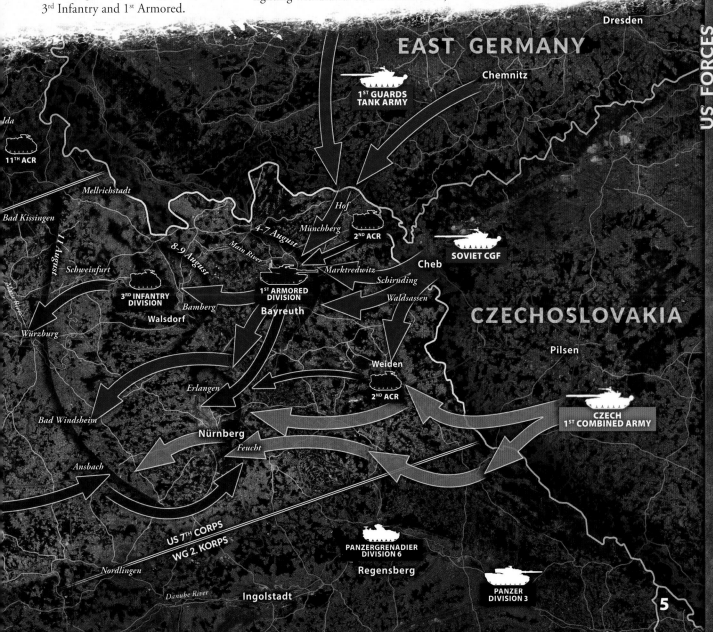

With the 3rd Infantry Division remaining in the line on the Main River, the 1st Infantry and 1st Armored were joined by the 82nd Airborne Division, freshly arrived from the United States, to take part in CENTAG's counterassault into East Germany. The initial phase of the offensive had taken elements of the West German 3. Korps and US 5th Corps over the inner German border. On 13 August elements of the US 7th Corps began crossing the border in the area of Mellrichstadt, taking over the positions of a West German panzergrenadier division. Their ultimate goal was the city of Leipzig in the heart of Saxony, East Germany.

Leading the way was the 1st Infantry Division who had to negotiate 20 km of forested hill country to Ilmenau on the East German side of the border. Resistance was light, but well-concealed. Most of 13 August was spent by the 'Big Red One' combing through the hills, rooting out pockets of resistance, and securing roads running northeast towards Erfurt. They faced a mix of Soviet second line motor infantry and East German border troops.

Meanwhile, the 3rd Infantry Division had advanced from the Main River to Bamberg, pushing Soviet forces back towards Bayreuth, securing the offensive's right flank.

To secure Ilmenau as the 1st Infantry Division worked through the hills, the 82nd Airborne Division landed a helicopter-borne force east of Ilmenau. They quickly took the town and captured its small East German garrison. With the hills secured, the 1st Armored Division was released to pass down on to the relatively flat country around Erfurt and Weimar.

ACROSS THURINGIA

The 1st Infantry Division dropped back to reserve and the 1st Armored Division then led the advance through East Germany towards the Saale River marking the border between the old German states of Thuringia and Saxony-Anhalt. One brigade of the 82nd Airborne Division, in the air assault role mounted in UH-1 Iriquois 'Huey' helicopters, operated in several Task Forces ahead of the 1st Armored Division's advance. Their role was to capture key river crossings and other

possible terrain bottle necks after they had been designated by the divisional cavalry of both divisions.

The advance took the lead elements of the 7th Corps northeast into the rolling countryside along the axis running through Stadtilm, Kranichfeld and Blankenhain. By the afternoon of 14 August the advance had run into resistance at Magdala. A sharp engagement between the advance element of the 1st Armored Division's divisional cavalry and Soviet recon troops was quickly broken off. Further probing across the Magdal River found only pockets of defending Warsaw Pact troops, and an attack was launched to the south of Mellingen. It had broken through the thinly held position by the evening.

The advance continued cautiously through the night and into the next day, heading past the hill country that surrounded the city of Jena to the east and towards the town of Apolda. Reconnaissance soon discovered that the Soviets had heavily reinforced positions running from Weimar to Apolda and Saaleplatte. The 7th Corps pushed an armoured force from the 1st Armored Division through the open fields between Apolda and Saaleplatte. The force burst through the Soviet line south of Utenbach, while US mech infantry forces engaged and held Soviet forces on either flank.

The breakthrough armoured force then pushed in the direction of the town of Bad Sulza, but were hit by a flanking Soviet counterattack from Niedertrebra village, 4km north of Saaleplatte, on their left. The counterattacking Soviets, with supporting attack helicopters, initially caused considerable casualties to the armoured task force before they were able to re-orientate themselves and respond. A savage encounter was fought for over an hour before the Soviets were finally forced to withdraw back past Niedertrebra and its adjacent villages.

In the meantime, mech infantry forces had broken through the rest of the Soviet positions and were rapidly advancing northward to join the leading armoured force. Once more the armoured cavalry were sent forward, the next goal was to cross the Saale River. They needed to locate any favourable

crossings, either with intact bridges or locations for the corps's bridging units to establish new crossings.

By the end of 15 August it had been discovered that most of the bridges along the Saale, immediately east of the line of advance of the 7th Corps, had been destroyed by withdrawing Soviet forces. The Saale River itself was too wide for the M60 AVLB bridge laying tanks, so the engineer bridging units were called forward and work began on several crossing. The air assault helicopter-borne troops of the 82nd Airborne Division were sent across at these points to establish a bridgehead. They were soon followed by the mech infantry mounted in their amphibious M113 armoured personnel carriers (APCs).

Though the 7th Corps' positions along the Saale came under sporadic artillery fire during the night, no attempts were made by Warsaw Pact forces to directly attack the bridgeheads. By the morning of 16 August the tanks and other heavy equipment were crossing, joining the troops already across and continuing the advance towards Leipzig.

ON TO LEIPZIG

By the late-morning of 16 August the lead element of the 2nd Armored Cavalry Regiment, who had taken over in the vanguard of the 7th Corps after crossing the Saale River, entered the outskirts of the town of Naumburg. They found it abandoned by the Soviets and were instead greeted by

WEST GERMAN
3. KORPS

US
7TH CO

Mellrichs

scattered groups of East German civilians who welcomed them as liberators. Intelligence indicated the Soviets had withdrawn back towards Leipzig and were being reinforced with units arriving from the Soviet Union and Poland. The West German 3. Korps on the 7th Corps northern flank, and the US 5th Corps to the south, had also advanced into East Germany, though not as far as the 7th Corps. However, with the Soviets pulling back towards Leipzig the 7th Corps commander felt his flanks were safe and pushed on.

The 7th Corps' advance continued into the afternoon, with the 2nd Armored Cavalry Regiment and 1st Armored Division pushing hard through the Saxon countryside. A few hours after taking Naumburg, US troops had entered Weißenfels, a further 10km northeast. The advance followed Autobahn 9, leading in the direction of Leipzig. Helicopter cavalry scouts, flying ahead of the ground cavalry, reported in the late afternoon enemy activity in the vicinity of Lützen, with positions running from the south of Leipzig, through Lützen, and northwards towards Merseburg.

With the enemy located, and the sun setting, air strikes and artillery were called in. While the Air Force and artillery pounded the Soviet positions, the corps commander set about organ-ising his forces to launch an attack to break through Soviet positions towards Leipzig. Three armour heavy brigades from the 1st Armored and 1st Infantry Divisions would be committed to attack along both sides of Autobahn 9 running through the gap between the Saale River and Lützen. Two mech-anised brigades would secure the towns on either flank. The attack was to be launched at 0300 hours under the cover of night, where the US forces' superior night-fighting technology would prove its worth.

BATTLE OF LÜTZEN
(ALSO SEE PAGE 8)

The 7th Corps attacked at 0300 hours on 17 August. The attack was led by the brigades of the 1st Armored Division, with the 1st Infantry Division in support. The main thrust of the advance headed towards Lützen and along Autobahn 9. The corps deployed the 82nd Airborne and 3rd Infantry divi-sions in reserve on the left and right.

Soviet defences were scattered among the villages that surrounded Lützen, using the ample cover including tree lines, small woods, and village buildings.

The battle was fought in darkness, the Americans fighting the Soviets village by village, running the gauntlet of small arms, tank, and missile fire. By the morning the autobahn had been secured as far north as Tollwitz and the town of Lützen had been taken. As the sun rose across the fields, lead elements of the 7th Corps could see their objec-tive ahead of them, the city of Leipzig.

LEIPZIG

With their objective in sight, the wheeled, tracked and airborne scouts of the 7th Corps were once more pushing out ahead of the main bodies to locate Warsaw Pact positions and formations, identifying targets for the Air Force and the corps artillery.

Probes into the outskirts of Leipzig discovered it to be lightly defended. Sporadic fighting broke out as rear guard Soviet units sprung delaying ambushes, before withdrawing and dispersing back amongst the city build-ings. The rest of the days fighting took its toll on both sides, until it subsided with the fall of dusk. By the morning of 18 August resistance had faded away to nothing. Further scouting discovered most of the Soviet and Warsaw Pact forces had withdrawn north-eastwards.

With Leipzig secure and corps' forces probing beyond, the 7th Corps was given a new objective, Berlin. NATO forces to the north and south of the corps had advanced and were posed to push on to the East German capital. It seemed more days of fighting lay ahead for the soldiers of the US 7th Corps.

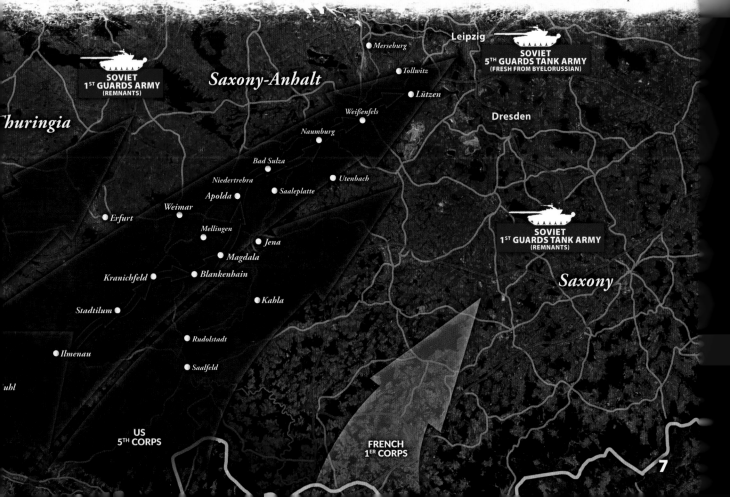

The 1st Armored Division had been in the thick of the fighting since the launch of 7th Corps' attack into East Germany on 13 August. By 17 August they were in sight of their final objective, Leipzig. One final push through Lützen would take them within striking distance.

The attack got underway at 0300 hours, shortly after Soviet positions were attacked with artillery and aircraft. The advance was led by the 1st and 2nd Brigades of the 1st Armored Division from just northeast of Weißenfels, with the 2nd Brigade of the 1st Infantry Division immediately behind ready to reinforce. The 1st and 3rd Brigades of the 1st Infantry Division protected the flanks and set about clearing the urban areas. The 1st Armored Division's 3rd Brigade stood by in immediate reserves. The corps deployed the 82nd Airborne and 3rd Infantry divisions in reserve on the left and right.

RIPPACH STREAM

The first engagement took place as the lead brigade approached a line of villages that ran westwards along the Rippach Stream towards the Saale River. From the cover of the villages, the Soviets unleashed a hail of tank and guided missile fire in the darkness. US tanks along the front started exploding and illuminating the night. Return fire was rapid and deadly and very quickly Soviet vehicles were burning throughout the villages.

The brigades' mech infantry advanced on foot and began clearing the villages. After about 20 minutes of heavy fighting the tanks were once more able to advance, pushing through the burning wrecks in the villages and on into the fields beyond.

The 1st Brigade, 1st Armored pushed northwards parallel to Autobahn 9, while the 2nd Brigade, 1st Armored followed the secondary road towards Lützen. The 1st Brigade, 1st Infantry and 3rd Brigade, 1st Infantry advanced up the flanks. The 1st Brigade, 1st Infantry took a succession of villages on the banks of the Saale River, while 3rd Brigade, 1st Infantry swung through Starsiedel to approach Lützen directly from the south.

RÖCKEN, MICHLITZ, AND BOTHFELD

The leading armoured brigades ran into more Soviet forces as they approached the three villages of Röcken, Michlitz, and Bothfeld about 2km southwest of Lützen.

The IPM1 Abrams tanks of 2nd Brigade, 1st Armored were met with a volley of anti-tank missiles as they approached through the gloom of the night. Several Abrams took hits, but only a couple were knocked out. Through their thermal imaging scopes they could see the Soviet infantry moving between the houses, trees, and their BMP-2 infantry fighting vehicles. The 2nd of the 37th Armored Battalion returned fire, while mech infantry and tanks from the other battalions worked around the flanks of the Soviet position. The US and Soviet infantry soon became embroiled in short range firefights around the outskirts of the villages, while the tanks picked off the BMPs as they found them. The improved armour of the new IPM1 Abrams proved its worth during the close-quarters fighting, with the Soviet infantry's RPGs and BMP 30mm cannons unable to penetrate even the side armour. The positions became bogged down in fighting for over an hour and it wasn't until around 0430 hours that positions could be declared secure.

KLEINKORBETHA AND OEBLES-SCHLECHTEWITZ

West of the 2nd Brigade, 1st Armored's battle, the 1st Brigade, 1st Armored was hit by an ambush as they advanced past the villages of Kleinkorbetha and Oebles-Schlechtewitz near the Saale River. A number of their M60 Patton tanks went up in flames. The advance was brought to a halt and the TOW and Dragon missiles were quickly brought made ready. The US tankers immediately searched the frontages of the two villages for enemy. A number of Soviet tanks could be seen in the darkness, the heat of their engines and gun barrels giving away their positions. Returning American tank and missile fire began raking the villages and Soviet tanks across the position began to burn. Once in position, the anti-tank missile teams and vehicles joined the fusillade. After several minutes of fire the Soviet tanks began to withdraw, pulling out of the village and retiring northwards in the direction of next village.

ELLERBACH STREAM

1st Brigade, 1st Armored then pushed on past the villages and turned northeast, following the direction of Autobahn 9 as it curved towards the north of Leipzig and leaving the completion of the villages' clearing to following brigades. After advancing about 1km they began to close on another row of villages at about 0400 hours, these hugging the Ellerbach Stream. The infantry approached on foot, while the tanks and M901 ITV missile vehicles sat back and waited to give fire support if required. South of them the 2nd Brigade, 1st Armored's battle could be heard raging around Röcken, Michlitz, and Bothfeld.

The infantry began infiltrating the row of villages from Tollwitz southeast across the autobahn to Zöllschen and Ellerbach. However, they found the Soviet motor riflemen occupying the villages alert to their approach and were greeted with bursts of machine-gun fire across their front. Heavy weapons joined in and the mech infantry were forced to halt their advance and seek cover. The M60 tanks and ITVs returned fire and began knocking out the vehicles that were giving fire support to the Soviet motor riflemen. The exchange lasted 10 minutes or so, with vehicles on both sides going up in flames as the battle intensified.

Two companies of 1st of the 37th Armor Battalion launched an attack around the southern flank of the villages past Ellerbach, where they encountered a battalion of Soviet T-64 tanks, who seemed poised to launch a counter-attack of their own. A running battle soon developed, the big M60 Pattons dwarfing the compact T-64 tanks. The T-64's more powerful gun and better armour was countered by the M60 Patton's superior night vision equipment. Fought at short ranges due to

the darkness, the 1st of the 37th Armor Battalion drove through the Soviet tanks' position, swinging behind their opponents. The battle raged for just a few short minutes, but the battlefield was left littered with destroyed and disabled tanks. The 1st of the 37th Armor Battalion withdrew, leaving about a quarter of its number behind. However, the Soviet tanks were in no condition to follow up and also withdrew.

In the meantime, the 1st of the 6th Mech Infantry Battalion had begun to make progress into the villages, securing Ellerbach and Zöllschen to the east of the autobahn, and had launched an attack across the autobahn into Ragwitz. Fighting continued for another half an hour with key buildings in the village exchanging hands on several occasions. By about 0510 hours the Soviet infantry had been pushed back to Tollwitz. The mech infantry and a company of supporting tanks continued to push west into Tollwitz and eventually the Soviet withdrew towards Bad Dürrenberg. With the 1st Infantry Division's flank brigade arriving from the south, the 1st Brigade, 1st Armored Division was free to continue along the autobahn.

LÜTZEN

South of Lützen, 2nd Brigade, 1st Armored pushed on to Lützen, with 3rd Brigade, 1st Infantry Division to their right. With the villages of Röcken, Michlitz, and Bothfeld secured behind them, the mech infantry of the brigades began working their way into Lützen, approaching it from the southwest.

The Soviets had taken positions among the houses and buildings that lined the road leading to the town centre. Missiles began streaking from the houses as Soviet infantry and BMPs engaged the advancing tanks and APCs. Soon the field to the west of Lützen was illuminated with scattered burning M113s. However, the mech infantry, already dismounted, quickly began assaulting the Soviet positions in response. In the darkness, the fighting for the town was savage and bloody, with much of it fought as close quarters. The US mech infantry slowly pushed the Soviets back and out of Lützen.

As the sun peaked its way over the horizon, the men of the 1st Armored Division pushed on to Leipzig.

1ST ARMORED DIVISION

1st 'Old Ironsides' Armored Division was the first division of the US armored forces. It was formed from the expanded 7th Cavalry Brigade in July 1940 and became the template which set the standard for the newly created armoured divisions. It was organised in two armoured regiments and one armoured infantry regiment, along with supporting artillery, engineers, and reconnaissance.

The division's nickname 'Old Ironsides' was chosen by its first commanding officer, General Magruder, in honour of the USS Constitution, one of the first warships of the United States Navy. Magruder appreciated the parallel between the famous warship that founded the US Navy and the 1st Armored Division setting the standard for the new armoured divisions.

The division took part in the American's first battles in North Africa, taking part in Operation Torch, landing at Oran on 8 November 1942 and liberating Algeria. They then fought in the battles for Tunisia, before they landed at Salerno in Italy in September 1943 and fought up Italy to the Winter and Gustav Lines. A year of tough fighting followed through the mountainous country, before they took part in the landings at Anzio in January 1944 followed by the final capture of Rome on 5 June 1944.

In July 1944, Old Ironsides reorganised and did away with the regimental structure, once more setting the standard for the organisation of the other armoured divisions for the rest of WWII. By the war's end Old Ironsides had crossed the Po River in the far north of Italy, finally completing the task it began three years earlier. The Germans had been broken.

After WWII Old Ironsides returned home to be the only combat-ready armoured division in the continental United States. It was one of the first Army divisions to integrate African-American soldiers throughout the ranks and the first to receive the M48 Patton Tank in 1953. Training for nuclear war was intensified in the mid-1950s.

Though Old Ironsides as a whole didn't participate in the Vietnam War, an aviation company and cavalry squadron did serve. In addition, in 1967 the 198th Infantry Brigade was formed from three of the division's infantry battalions and deployed to Vietnam.

As part of the post-Vietnam reorganisation, the 1st Armored Division was moved to West Germany in 1971 where it replaced the 4th Armored Division in the Bavarian city of Ansbach. The division became part of the US 7th Corps, itself part of NATO's Central Army Group (CENTAG).

1st Battalion, 51st Infantry (Mech), part of the 1st Brigade, was made inactive on 16 June 1984. This was a result of the division's conversion to the Division 86 force structure. The 1st 'Old Ironsides' Armored Division under the new organisation has a total of six armour battalions and four mechanised infantry battalions. Most of the division had completed the conversion to the new organisation by 1984. These are divided amongst three mixed brigades, as the division's general sees fit.

The regiment numbers of the United States Army Regimental System (eg. '37th Armored Regiment') seem strange and arbitrary at first. This is because, in the modern era, the regiment is no longer important as an organisational unit. Each battalion is still affiliated with a regiment, but only ceremonially. For actual organisational purposes, the battalion is part of the brigade, and then the division to which it belongs.

The 1st Armored Division is also in a state of transition with its equipment; some battalions having changed to the M1 or IPM1 Abrams, while some units still fight in the older M60A3 main battle tank. The mech battalions were equipped with M113 APCs and ITV anti-tank missile vehicles.

Captain William 'Buck' Taylor's combat team had been on edge for the last few days. They'd been put on alert about a week ago and had just finished moving to their forward positions in the passes north of Bayreuth, near Himmelkron. Buck watched on as the boys from the maintenance section fussed around the new IPM1 Abrams tanks, checking and rechecking things.

"Red, they'll be fine," Buck called across to the chief mechanic, Sergeant Red Fergusson, "we've had them for months with no trouble."

"Just making sure, it's better to be safe than sorry, that's what my old ma' use to say, Cap'," came Red's reply.

Buck, a nickname he'd earned during his basic training after an unfortunate incident with a bar's mechanical bull, commanded A Company of the 2nd Battalion, 37th Armored Regiment, or '2nd of the 37th' in US Army parlance. The battalion, along with the rest of the 2nd Brigade, 1st Armored Division, had moved from Ferris Barracks in Erlangen to their positions near Bayreuth on 27 July. The commies, if they came, were expected to attack through the Hof Corridor around the picturesque town of Hof and then on towards the hill passes leading to the Weißer Main River valley.

North-west of Himmelkron the brigade had prepared several positions covering the main approaches through the hills on the southern edge of the Frankenwald range.

The 2nd of the 37th had its battalion headquarters in Himmelkron, with each of its three companies in positions around the villages of Marktschorgast, Wasserknoden, and Hohenknoden, covering the roads that lead down to the Weißer Main River valley. The battalion's fourth company had been attached out in exchange for a mech infantry company from the 2nd of the 6th Mech (2nd Battalion, 6th Mech Infantry Regiment).

A Company had been assigned a mech platoon (Lieutenant James Kozlowski), making the company 'Combat Team Alpha'. Captain Buck Taylor's Team Alpha was positioned around Marktschorgast, covering Autobahn 9. The mech platoon had set up positions in a farm near the entrance to the Autobahn pass. The three tank platoons were in concealing positions facing east, 1st Platoon, under Lieutenant Andy Haught, occupied the edge of a wood facing Autobahn 9 and the road to Marktschorgast. Lieutenant Robert Vertoli's 2nd Platoon were positioned in the village of Falls, while 3rd Platoon, commanded by Lieutenant Don Andersen, deployed nestled in a tree line running along a railroad line west of Falls.

Out ahead of the brigade the divisional cavalry had push forward, joining the squadron of the 2nd Armored Cavalry Regiment stationed on the inner German border near Hof.

MARKTSCHORGAST

As the evening of 3 August set in the men of Combat Team Alpha took up their shifts on watch and settled in for another night of waiting, peering out into the darkness searching for anything out of the ordinary. So far it had been pretty ordinary, the village was quiet, as most of the locals had packed up their cars and headed west. They had seen the TV and newspapers and knew things were not good, something was about to go off. The soldiers of Buck's combat team had also sensed a palpable tension among the officers, it seemed this might actually be war.

In Team Alpha's HQ, set up in a house at the edge of the town, Buck gathered his platoon leaders and had them mark the fall back locations on their map, before he headed off to the battalion HQ for the evening meeting with the CO.

The night passed without incident, and all seemed quiet until an hour before dawn when the distinct sound of artillery thumping in the distance breeched the silence. Soon after, battalion HQ radioed Buck and he learned the Soviets had begun bombarding a number of the 2nd Armored Cavalry Regiment's positions along the front. His combat team was ordered to full alert. He quickly contacted each of his platoons and in only few minutes each platoon leader had his tanks and men ready for action. His own IPM1 tank and crew were organised by his ever efficient gunner, Sergeant Bobby Découx, and ready before he left his HQ. XO Lieutenant Carl Jackson's crew were not far behind.

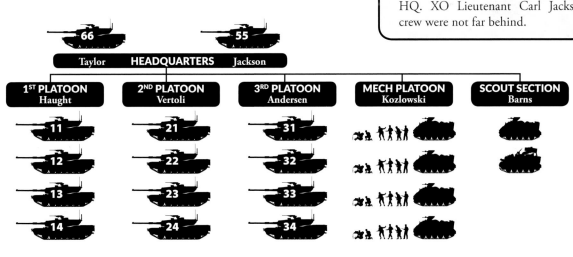

COMBAT TEAM ALPHA
A Company, 2nd Battalion, 37th Armored Regiment

It was about 1100 hours when Captain Buck Taylor's combat team finally sighted the enemy. Surprisingly is wasn't the expected screen of recon troops, but tanks and infantry fighting vehicles. Team Alpha's attached scout section out front of their positions had radioed that a tank formation had pushed past Münchberg and to expect a sizable force at any time. And it was.

About five minutes after the withdrawing scout section had passed through, Lieutenant Haught spotted a tank emerging in the area of the bend in the autobahn. It was quickly followed by several more. These were a relatively close 400 metres away. Haught ordered his platoon to concentrate on the targets around the autobahn, he was sure Lieutenant Vertoli's platoon would take care of the tanks coming from north of the autobahn.

Vertoli had indeed spotted the T-64 tanks advancing across the fields north of the autobahn.

"Hold fire until my word," he ordered across his platoon net.

He waited until eight tanks had crested the slight rise in the distance.

"Engage targets." His four tanks immediately opened fire. The crews worked smoothly and sent the first volley of rounds into the enemy tanks. Three tanks took hits, but only two started to burn. The third shook and bounced, but remained in action. Vertoli could see from the short 600 metres away that the shot had left a shiny gouge on the hull front.

"These may take a few boys. Fire at will Jones," Vertoli instructed his gunner.

The platoon continued to plug away at the T-64s. Another three T-64 were taken out. Return fire peppered around the village's edge, but it seemed the Soviet tankers were having trouble locating the platoon. A shot slammed into Sergeant Grayson's IPM1 tank and it rocked back.

"2 2 Report," Vertoli called to Grayson.

"Roger 2 1, we're ok, ears are ringing. Frost banged his jaw on the breech when it hit, bit of blood but he'll be fine. He may have soiled himself. I'm not sure if our old M60 would have taken that," Grayson reported on his crew, injured loader, and tank.

"Relocate, they probably have your position," the Lieutenant instructed.

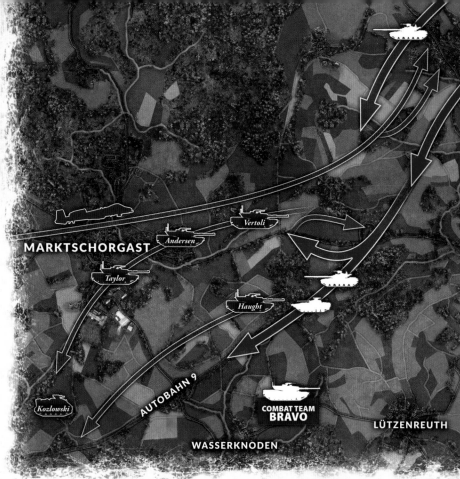

Another three T-64s had joined the three remaining from the first wave and the firefight continued.

Meanwhile, Lieutenant Haught's platoon had been firing on the tanks and APCs approaching around the autobahn, with about half a dozen heading up the Marktschorgast link road. They picked off the tanks first, but the T-64 tanks, as Corporal Yates identified from the tiny road wheels, were proving tough nuts to crack. Less than half of the hits from their IPM1's 105mm guns were penetrating. However, being nestled among the trees of the woodland allowed the US tanks to keep firing with little in the way of accurate return fire. After about three minutes of fire an enemy round hit and penetrated. Lieutenant Haught noticed a streak to his left then Corporal Yates's tank was engulfed in flames and dust.

"1 4 check," silence was all that greeted Lieutenant Haught query. He quickly switched to concern for his other tanks, "missiles, relocate to fall-back one."

The IPM1 Abrams tanks backed out of their position and took the nearby forest track toward their predesignated first fall-back position near the farm the mech platoon had occupied. Main gun and missile rounds continued to fall around them as they moved out, leaving the sad sight of Tank 14 in the

trees. They slowly drove along the dirt track, keeping their speed down to avoid creating a noticeable dust cloud. A thump was heard on Lieutenant Haught's tank hull, and he turned to look. Clambering on to the back of the turret were the four crewmen of Tank 14, Corporal Yates was grinning at him. All four looked singed and they all had cuts on their exposed skin.

"The fire suppression system works sir," came Corporal Yates's answer to his unasked question.

They continued on to the road running parallel to the autobahn then across the fields to the farm.

Captain Buck Taylor, watching on from his positions on the edge of Marktschorgast spotted the Soviet tanks heading his way from the autobahn. He warned Andersen's 3rd Tank Platoon to watch the flank, and ordered Vertoli to be prepared to withdraw from Falls towards Marktschorgast.

Both the HQ and Andersen's IPM1 Abrams fired on the Soviet tanks advancing up the Marktschorgast road. A round from Jackson's tank slammed into the lead T-64 as it cross the railroad level crossing and it jerked to a halt and rolled into a ditch. A volley of shots from Andersen's platoon hit the flank of the rear of the Soviet tank column, knocking out two more tanks. The remaining three T-64s turned towards Andersen's positions and fired. The shots peppered the tree line, and Tank 33 took a hit through the left track and drive sprocket. Further rounds from Andersen's and Vertoli's tanks zeroed in on the T-64s, destroying another, and the remaining two began retreating towards the autobahn.

To further delay the Soviet advance and buy some time for his combat team to withdraw to the autobahn pass Buck requested an air strike. Meanwhile, Andersen and Vertoli withdrew their platoons back through Marktschorgast and then towards the autobahn pass.

A flight of A-10s roared over 10 minutes later, just as the Soviets had advanced past Falls and were closing in on Marktschorgast, and a streak of Maverick missiles smashed into the leading formation of T-64 tanks. As the A-10s wheeled away the left a line of burning wrecks in their wake. Lines of tracer fire could be seen coming from the Soviet Shilka anti-aircraft tanks firing as the A-10s flew over.

AUTOBAHN PASS

The air strike had done its job and Buck's combat team were now ensconced in their fall back positions around the entrance to the autobahn pass that lead down to the town of Himmelkron. There they were joined by Combat Team Bravo (B Company), while Combat Team Charlie (C Company) held the forestry tracks and road that lead down to Gössenreuth.

Several more attempts were made by the lead element of the Soviet armoured force to break past the positions in the autobahn pass, each meeting fierce resistance from the companies of the 2nd of the 37th, supporting artillery from positions near Himmelkron, and marauding Cobra attack helicopters and A-10 Warthog strike aircraft. During the night engineers moved in and ripped up the tracks on the railroad on the cutting about the autobahn, as well as mining the autobahn.

In the early hours of 5 August the 2nd of the 37th was relieved by the 2nd Battalion, 81st Armor Regiment (2nd of the 81st) and the battalion was immediately ordered to the Autobahn 70 gap in the hills east of Harsdorf, one of several roads leading through the hills on west side of the Weißer Main River valley leading to Bayreuth. There they were to prepare new defensive positions, receive replacements, and resupply.

2nd of the 81st held the pass east of Himmelkron into the afternoon, eventually falling back through Himmelkron along the route of Autobahn 9 toward the pass west of Benk that the autobahn shared with Bundestrasse 2 (Federal Road 2). Not far behind them the Soviets streamed out of passes along the Weißer Main River, some had passes had held, but once one blocking position had been forced to withdraw, the rest of the US forces began their retreat to new positions on the western side of the valley.

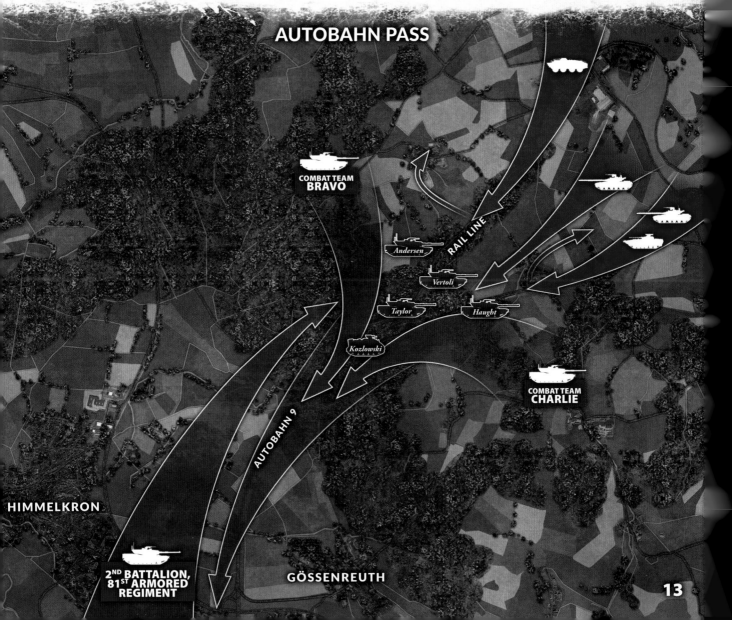

AUTOBAHN PASS

COMBAT TEAM BRAVO

Andersen

RAIL LINE

Vertoli

Taylor

Haught

Kozlowski

COMBAT TEAM CHARLIE

AUTOBAHN 9

HIMMELKRON

2ND BATTALION, 81ST ARMORED REGIMENT

GÖSSENREUTH

KREMITZ

Andersen

Vertoli

Kozlowski

LETTENHOF

Taylor

Haught

AUTOBAHN 9

HARSDORF

COMBAT TEAM BRAVO

NENNTMANNSREUTH

FIRST BATTLE OF LETTENHOF

Meanwhile, the 2nd of the 37th stood ready east of Harsdorf covering Autobahn 70. Captain 'Buck' Taylor's Team Alpha had received replacement tanks for the two that had been lost. Corporal Yates and the crew of Tank 14, despite some burns and cuts, were raring to get back into action, they immediately christened their new tank 14A, 'Avenger'. The crew from Andersen's platoon, who had lost Tank 33 to disabled running gear, counted themselves lucky, but were disappointed they weren't able to recover the tank for repairs before the Soviets overran the position. Unlike Lieutenant Haught, Andersen would have no truck with names for his tanks, so like its predecessor, the new tank became 33.

The tank platoons were positioned on the ridge east of Lettenhof covering Autobahn 9 as it emerged from Kremitz, as well as the interchange between Autobahn 9 and 70. It was about 1800 hours when the first Soviets came from north of Kremitz,

a group of scout cars appeared from the village, spread out into the fields, and began advancing along the road towards Lettenhof. Meanwhile, behind them T-64 tanks and BMPs were advancing east of Autobahn 9 through Kremitz. Buck's Team Alpha began firing on the Soviet T-64s and BMPs to their east, having immediate effect as they caught a fair number of the tanks in the flank. BMPs and T-64s were left burning throughout the Soviet formation. Team Alpha was joined by Team Bravo when the Soviets passed Kremitz and turned south.

As the BMPs kept advancing, the T-64 tanks turned to face the US combat teams. They returned fire sending 122mm rounds towards the positions of Teams Alpha and Bravo, plastering the positions with rounds, most of which missed the well-concealed IPM1 Abrams tanks.

Four Mi-24 Hind attack helicopters emerged from behind Kremitz and made a run on Team Alpha, launching a volley of AT-6 Spiral missiles. The guided missiles ploughed into Vertoli's platoon position.

Clumps of earth and vegetation sprayed into the air all around as an explosion rocked Tank 22.

"Tank 22, report," Vertoli called to his number two tank.

"Lost engine, ammunition blow out, crew fine, over," reported Sergeant White.

The Hinds roared off over Team Alpha and on to Lettenhof where they were hit by a stream of tracer fire from beyond the village. The division had stationed a platoon of M247 Sergeant York anti-aircraft tanks in the gully leading down from Lettenhof to Harsdorf. The twin 40mm Bofors guns of the Sergeant Yorks had torn through two of the four Hinds, sending one spiralling into a nearby wood, while the second turned back to their lines, billowing black smoke while slowly losing altitude.

As the US fire took its toll, the Soviets began withdrawing south-east towards Neudorf and Bundesstrasse 2, dogged by harassing fire from Team Alpha and Bravo. Further attempts by the Soviets to break the 2nd Brigade's line defending the approaches to Bayreuth lasted into the night, finally abating in the early hours of 6 August.

SECOND BATTLE OF LETTENHOF

At around 0600 hours, artillery and rocket fire began falling on the positions of Team Alpha, shredding camouflage and tearing up the ground around the tanks. Tank crews were quick to seek refuge in their vehicles as the barrage blasted the area around them. Ten minutes later the barrage ended as quickly as it started. Captain Taylor's crews set about clearing debris from vision devices and checking the tanks for damage. Buck was receiving a report from Lieutenant Vertoli over the company net when Lieutenant Jackson called over from his nearby tank.

"Here they come again," Jackson pointed east to the wooded area adjacent to Autobahn 9.

Emerging from the woods were a large number of Soviet infantry trailing behind a line of BMP-2 infantry fighting vehicles. As Buck watched on, a number of the BMPs halted. Already his crews were scrambling back into their tanks, while Lieutenant Kozlowski's infantry trained their automatic weapons on the advancing riflemen and their

M47 Dragon anti-tank missiles on the BMPs, waiting for the right shot. One of the stationary BMPs let loose its AT-5 Spandrel missile towards the combat team's position. As it did three streaks fizzed out from Kozlowski's position as his Dragon teams sent three missile towards the stationary BMPs. The AT-5 struck Tank 22, which was un-crewed and waiting for a recovery team to come and retrieve it, hitting it squarely in the front and not doing any further damage to the already disabled tank. The three Dragon missiles struck three BMPs in quick succession and made burning wrecks of all three vehicles. The platoon's M249 SAWs opened up once the infantry got within 500 metres of their positions.

Meanwhile, Team Alpha's tanks had been knocking out the advancing BMPs, leaving smoking wrecks scattered about the fields. Taylor called in artillery, and soon 155m howitzer rounds were falling among the Soviet riflemen. The Soviet advance faltered, some men hit the deck, while others began heading back towards more substantial cover in nearby tree lines and ditches. The few remaining BMPs soon

backed off, retiring into the wood from which they came.

Probes continued throughout the day, some from the north, more from the east. All across the front elements of the Soviet 1st Guards Tank Army attempted to break the positions of the 1st Armored Division, but like their nickname, they continued to prove they too had ironsides.

WITHDRAWAL

As pressure mounted, and Czech forces joined from the south-east, the decision was made by the corps commander to begin withdrawing towards Erlangen and Nürnberg and defend the hills and forests east of these cities (the Franconian Jura upland).

Team Alpha and Captain Buck Taylor had much more fighting ahead of them. They would spend another four days in the defence of northern Bavaria before their division was relieved by the French. They would then move north to take part in the 7th Corps's offensive into East Germany.

SECOND BATTLE OF LETTENHOF

KREMITZ

Andersen

Vertoli

Kozlowski

Taylor

LETTENHOF

Haught

AUTOBAHN 9

NENNTMANNSREUTH

RSDORF

COMBAT TEAM BRAVO

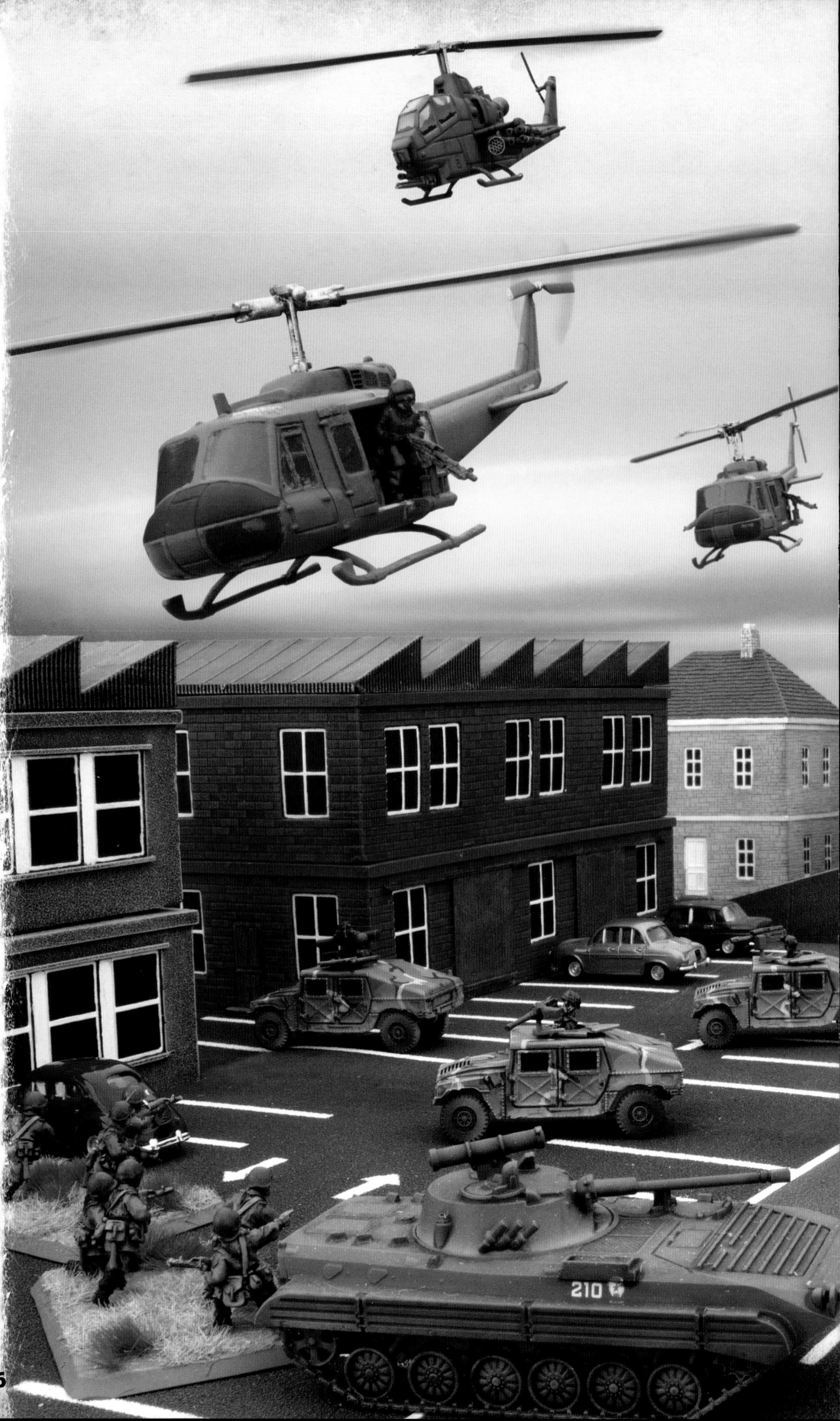
210

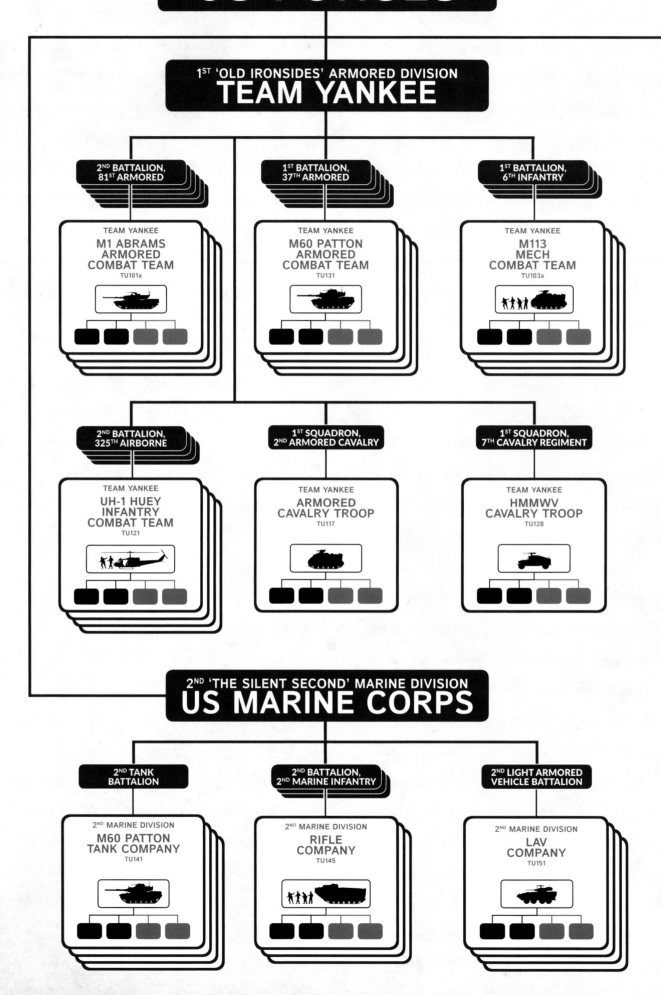

US FORCES

1ST 'OLD IRONSIDES' ARMORED DIVISION
TEAM YANKEE

2ND BATTALION, 81ST ARMORED

TEAM YANKEE
M1 ABRAMS ARMORED COMBAT TEAM
TU101a

1ST BATTALION, 37TH ARMORED

TEAM YANKEE
M60 PATTON ARMORED COMBAT TEAM
TU131

1ST BATTALION, 6TH INFANTRY

TEAM YANKEE
M113 MECH COMBAT TEAM
TU103a

2ND BATTALION, 325TH AIRBORNE

TEAM YANKEE
UH-1 HUEY INFANTRY COMBAT TEAM
TU121

1ST SQUADRON, 2ND ARMORED CAVALRY

TEAM YANKEE
ARMORED CAVALRY TROOP
TU117

1ST SQUADRON, 7TH CAVALRY REGIMENT

TEAM YANKEE
HMMWV CAVALRY TROOP
TU128

2ND 'THE SILENT SECOND' MARINE DIVISION
US MARINE CORPS

2ND TANK BATTALION

2ND MARINE DIVISION
M60 PATTON TANK COMPANY
TU141

2ND BATTALION, 2ND MARINE INFANTRY

2ND MARINE DIVISION
RIFLE COMPANY
TU145

2ND LIGHT ARMORED VEHICLE BATTALION

2ND MARINE DIVISION
LAV COMPANY
TU151

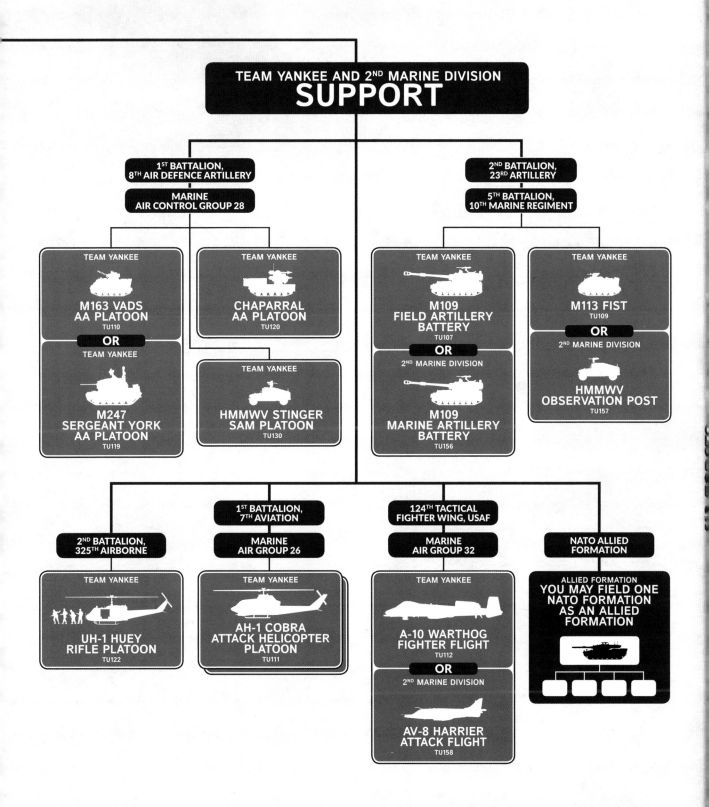

TEAM YANKEE AND 2ND MARINE DIVISION
SUPPORT

1ST BATTALION, 8TH AIR DEFENCE ARTILLERY

MARINE AIR CONTROL GROUP 28

TEAM YANKEE

M163 VADS AA PLATOON
TU110

OR

TEAM YANKEE

M247 SERGEANT YORK AA PLATOON
TU119

TEAM YANKEE

CHAPARRAL AA PLATOON
TU120

TEAM YANKEE

HMMWV STINGER SAM PLATOON
TU130

2ND BATTALION, 23RD ARTILLERY

5TH BATTALION, 10TH MARINE REGIMENT

TEAM YANKEE

M109 FIELD ARTILLERY BATTERY
TU107

OR

2ND MARINE DIVISION

M109 MARINE ARTILLERY BATTERY
TU156

TEAM YANKEE

M113 FIST
TU109

OR

2ND MARINE DIVISION

HMMWV OBSERVATION POST
TU157

2ND BATTALION, 325TH AIRBORNE

TEAM YANKEE

UH-1 HUEY RIFLE PLATOON
TU122

1ST BATTALION, 7TH AVIATION

MARINE AIR GROUP 26

TEAM YANKEE

AH-1 COBRA ATTACK HELICOPTER PLATOON
TU111

124TH TACTICAL FIGHTER WING, USAF

MARINE AIR GROUP 32

TEAM YANKEE

A-10 WARTHOG FIGHTER FLIGHT
TU112

OR

2ND MARINE DIVISION

AV-8 HARRIER ATTACK FLIGHT
TU158

NATO ALLIED FORMATION

ALLIED FORMATION
YOU MAY FIELD ONE NATO FORMATION AS AN ALLIED FORMATION

NATO ALLIED SUPPORT

Often divisions from other NATO nations, such as the West German divisions or the Canadian Brigade in CENTAG, fought alongside US Army Forces.

You can take an Allied Formation as part of your Force. An Allied Formation obeys all the rules for its own nationality. An Allied Formation Commander can only join Units in its own Formation and only its Formation Units can benefit from its Command Leadership (see page 25 and 64 of the rulebook).

An Allied Formation does not count as a Formation when counting how many Formations are left when determining if you have lost the game (see page 65 of the rulebook).

Recon was running hot out in front, so the M1 Abrams of 2nd platoon were moving fast with the Honeywell gas turbine engines whining in high gear. Three tanks crested and leapt over the slight ridge line, massive turrets rotating and the barrels of the 105mm cannons gently swaying as the stabilisers kept them focused for the gunners. The lead tank powered through the first farm, knocking fences over and exploding a hay bale into a golden cloud.

"Chambers! We're NOT the A-Team! Stop running over things!" Sergeant King berated his driver, but wasn't too concerned. According to the recon boys, enemy tanks were redeploying over the next rise. Catching them while on the move would present generous targets for his platoon.

There was no warning. A spark, a contrail and a resounding boom as an ATGM detonated against the turret of Corporal Pascal's tank. Bowers, his gunner, was already laying sights on the BMP-2 hiding behind a barn that had launched the missile. The gun thundered, and the enemy vehicle was knocked sideways, beginning to belch thick black smoke.

"Pascal! Status?" There was a moment's silence.

"Turret's locked. We're ok but combat ineffective. I'll head back. Good luck with the shoot." He sounded shaken up as his tank rotated in place before moving off towards base.

Corporal Wallen's tank followed King up to the crest, just two of them now. Down on the valley floor a column of five T-64's were pushing through abandoned vehicles on a bridge approach. Perfect targets. Both Abrams tanks fired. The lead tank stopped dead, a hole bored through its flank. The rear tank jerked sideways and guttered flames which flickered over the engine deck. The remaining T-64's dashed into cover as the Abrams reversed off the slope and began to move to new firing positions. Chambers began singing 'A View to a Kill' as he wrestled the tank towards the next firing location. Wallen got into position first, fired a shot, and withdrew.

"Missed. Last house on the left before the bridge."

King instructed Bowers on the target and then watched as Chambers eased them up until the Soviet tank was visible. The firing of the round and the explosion of the T-64 were almost simultaneous. Two on two now.

"Let's finish it. Driver - advance!"

The 1st 'Old Ironsides' Armored Division is a powerful combat force equipped with tried and tested kit like the M60A3 Patton tank and M113 armoured personnel carrier, as well as the latest in hi-tech equipment like the M1 and IPM1 Abrams tank.

The division fields three Brigades, each of these contain three or four mechanized infantry or armoured battalions. Like all of the heavy divisions (armoured or mechanized), the 1st Armored operates with a combined arms approach, pairing armoured battalions with mechanized infantry battalions and exchanging a company between them to form combined-arms task forces. The task forces then take the process a step further by swapping a platoon from their loaned company for one from one of their own companies to form a mixed company-sized 'combat team'. These can be either tank heavy in a Armored Combat Team, or mechanized infantry heavy in a Mech Combat Team. This gives the infantry some tank support, while giving the tanks the ability to hold or clear woods and towns with their attached infantry.

All of this puts a heavy responsibility on company commanders, but if they are up to it, the division reaps a good harvest. Each task force and combat team is a miniature army on its own, quite capable of tackling any sort of challenge. It is the combination of this mental and physical agility and massive supporting firepower that makes the heavy division such a deadly opponent.

AIRLAND BATTLE

Recognising that Soviet tactics could overwhelm them with sheer numbers, let alone the fact that Soviet tanks carried heavier guns than their own, the US Army developed the AirLand Battle concept. They would fight a mobile battle against the Soviet spearhead, while air, artillery, and special operation forces slowed the second echelon following behind. The result would stretch out the Warsaw Pact's advance in space and time, allowing the smaller NATO forces to continually attack the enemy all along the battlefront, while the reinforcements arrived piecemeal. This doctrine relied heavily on the initiative of junior officers in charge of the combat teams.

M1 ABRAMS ARMORED COMBAT TEAM

TEAM YANKEE

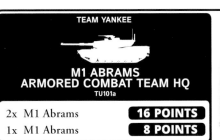

M1 ABRAMS
ARMORED COMBAT TEAM HQ
TU101a

2x M1 Abrams	**16 POINTS**
1x M1 Abrams	**8 POINTS**

OPTIONS

- Replace any or all M1 Abrams tanks with IPM1 Abrams tanks for +1 point each.

IPM1 Abrams tanks have Front armour 19 instead of 18, and Side armour 10 instead of 8.

• TANK FORMATION • CHOBHAM ARMOUR •
• THERMAL IMAGING •

COURAGE 3+	SKILL 3+
MORALE 3+	ASSAULT 4+
REMOUNT 2+	COUNTERATTACK 3+

IS HIT ON 4+			
	FRONT	SIDE	TOP
M1	18	8	2
IPM1	19	10	2

TACTICAL	TERRAIN DASH	CROSS COUNTRY DASH	ROAD DASH	CROSS
14"/35CM	18"/45CM	28"/70CM	32"/80CM	2+

WEAPON	RANGE	ROF HALTED	ROF MOVING	ANTI-TANK	FIRE-POWER	NOTES
M68 105mm gun	40"/100CM	2	2	20	2+	*Advanced Stabiliser, Laser Rangefinder*
.50 cal AA MG	20"/50CM	3	2	4	5+	
7.62mm AA MG	16"/40CM	1	1	2	6	
7.62mm MG	16"/40CM	1	1	2	6	

TEAM YANKEE

M1 ABRAMS
TANK PLATOON
TU102a

TEAM YANKEE

M1 ABRAMS
TANK PLATOON
TU102a

TEAM YANKEE

M106
HEAVY MORTAR
PLATOON
TU108

TEAM YANKEE

M901 ITV
ANTI-TANK
PLATOON
TU106

TEAM YANKEE

M1 ABRAMS
TANK PLATOON
TU102a

TEAM YANKEE

M113
MECH PLATOON
TU104

TEAM YANKEE

M113 SCOUT
SECTION
TU113

M1 ABRAMS TANK PLATOON

M1 ABRAMS TANK PLATOON

4x M1 Abrams	**32 POINTS**
3x M1 Abrams	**24 POINTS**
2x M1 Abrams	**16 POINTS**

OPTION
- Replace any or all M1 Abrams tanks with IPM1 Abrams tanks for +1 point each.

IPM1 Abrams tanks have Front armour 19 instead of 18, and Side armour 10 instead of 8.

• TANK UNIT • CHOBHAM ARMOUR •
• THERMAL IMAGING •

COURAGE 4+	SKILL 4+
MORALE 4+	ASSAULT 4+
REMOUNT 2+	COUNTERATTACK 4+

IS HIT ON 4+

	FRONT	SIDE	TOP
M1	18	8	2
IPM1	19	10	2

TACTICAL	TERRAIN DASH	CROSS COUNTRY DASH	ROAD DASH	CROSS
14"/35CM	18"/45CM	28"/70CM	32"/80CM	2+

WEAPON	RANGE	ROF HALTED	ROF MOVING	ANTI-TANK	FIRE-POWER	NOTES
M68 105mm gun	40"/100CM	2	2	20	2+	*Advanced Stabiliser, Laser Rangefinder*
.50 cal AA MG	20"/50CM	3	2	4	5+	
7.62mm AA MG	16"/40CM	1	1	2	6	
7.62mm MG	16"/40CM	1	1	2	6	

The M1 Abrams is America's first totally-new battle tank since the Second World War. Its top secret Chobham armour makes it one of the best protected tanks in the world, and one of the heaviest tanks. Despite this, its multi-fuel gas turbine engine makes it the fastest as well.

The M1 Abrams' NATO-standard 105mm gun fires the latest long-rod, fin-stabilised ammunition, giving it incredible penetrating power. This time-tested gun combines remarkably compact rounds for a high rate of fire, with a deadly effect against almost any type of target. Its advanced stabiliser, laser rangefinder, and thermal imager allow it to hit targets at any range while moving rapidly across any terrain, whether by day or by night.

Crew survivability is another focus of this superb design. The tank's ready-use ammunition is all stored in an armoured compartment at the back of the tank. If the ammunition is hit, blow-out panels on the top of the turret ensure the crews survival. If the tank doesn't blow up immediately when it's hit, the crew know they are safe to continue fighting.

Overall, the M1 Abrams is perhaps the best tank in existence, with a good balance between the triad of mobility, protection, and firepower.

In 1984, the IP (Improved Performance) M1 Abrams was produced and issued to a number of tank units. The IPM1 fitted a new turret with improved frontal armoured protection. The IPM1 Abrams included a number of other improvements including; new reinforced suspension, transmission modifications, improved armour protection, improved protection between the crew and ammunition storage, as well as the new turret.

Crew: 4 - commander, gunner, loader, driver
Weight: 55.70 tonnes
Length: 9.77m (32')
Width: 3.66m (12')
Height: 2.44m (8')
Weapons: M68 105mm Gun
M2HB .50 cal MG
2x M240 7.62mm MG
M1 Armour: Chobham - 42cm RHA equivalent, 65cm RHA against HEAT
IPM1 Armour: Chobham - 42cm RHA equivalent, 65cm RHA against HEAT
Speed: 72 km/h (45 mph)
Engine: Honeywell AGT1500C gas turbine 1,120 kW (1,500 hp)
Range: 480 km (300 miles)

M60 PATTON ARMORED COMBAT TEAM

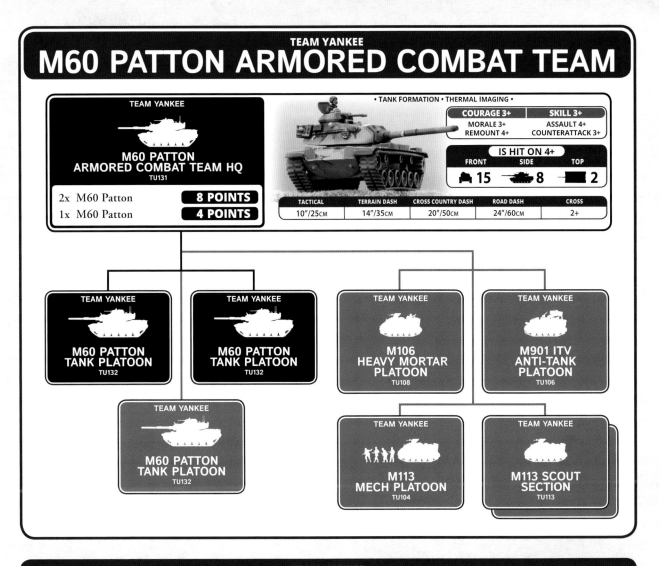

TEAM YANKEE

M60 PATTON ARMORED COMBAT TEAM HQ
TU131

| 2x M60 Patton | **8 POINTS** |
| 1x M60 Patton | **4 POINTS** |

• TANK FORMATION • THERMAL IMAGING •

COURAGE 3+	SKILL 3+
MORALE 3+	ASSAULT 4+
REMOUNT 4+	COUNTERATTACK 3+

IS HIT ON 4+

FRONT	SIDE	TOP
🚗 15	🛡 8	▬ 2

TACTICAL	TERRAIN DASH	CROSS COUNTRY DASH	ROAD DASH	CROSS
10"/25CM	14"/35CM	20"/50CM	24"/60CM	2+

TEAM YANKEE
M60 PATTON TANK PLATOON
TU132

TEAM YANKEE
M60 PATTON TANK PLATOON
TU132

TEAM YANKEE
M106 HEAVY MORTAR PLATOON
TU108

TEAM YANKEE
M901 ITV ANTI-TANK PLATOON
TU106

TEAM YANKEE
M60 PATTON TANK PLATOON
TU132

TEAM YANKEE
M113 MECH PLATOON
TU104

TEAM YANKEE
M113 SCOUT SECTION
TU113

M60 PATTON TANK PLATOON

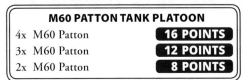

M60 PATTON TANK PLATOON	
4x M60 Patton	**16 POINTS**
3x M60 Patton	**12 POINTS**
2x M60 Patton	**8 POINTS**

The M60 Patton was introduced to the US Army in 1960 becoming the Army's first officially designated main battle tank, effectively bringing an end to the medium and heavy tank distinctions that had gone before.

Though based on the M48 Patton medium tank, the M60 included a number of significant improvements like the new M68 105mm gun, substantially more armour, and an improved power plant.

The M60A3 Patton tank was the final model and was in service with US Army tank units not yet upgraded with M1 Abrams. The M60A3 had undergone a number improvements over the M60A1 model (still in use by the US Marines) which included adding smoke dischargers, a laser-rangefinder that could be used by both commander and gunner, a ballistic computer, intergrated stabiliser, and thermal imaging night vision sights.

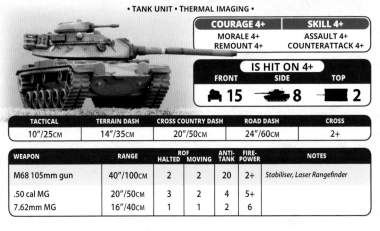

• TANK UNIT • THERMAL IMAGING •

COURAGE 4+	SKILL 4+
MORALE 4+	ASSAULT 4+
REMOUNT 4+	COUNTERATTACK 4+

IS HIT ON 4+

FRONT	SIDE	TOP
🚗 15	🛡 8	▬ 2

TACTICAL	TERRAIN DASH	CROSS COUNTRY DASH	ROAD DASH	CROSS
10"/25CM	14"/35CM	20"/50CM	24"/60CM	2+

WEAPON	RANGE	ROF HALTED	ROF MOVING	ANTI-TANK	FIRE-POWER	NOTES
M68 105mm gun	40"/100CM	2	2	20	2+	Stabiliser, Laser Rangefinder
.50 cal MG	20"/50CM	3	2	4	5+	
7.62mm MG	16"/40CM	1	1	2	6	

Crew: 4 - commander, gunner, loader, driver
Weight: 52.6 tonnes
Length: 9.309m (30' 6.5") (gun forward)
Width: 3.631m (11' 11")
Height: 3.213m (10' 6.5")
Weapons: M68 105mm Gun, M85 .50 cal MG, M73 7.62mm MG

Armour: Upper Glacis: 109mm (4.29") at 65° Turret Front: 250mm (10") equivalent
Speed: 72 km/h (45 mph)
Engine: Continental AVDS-1790-2 V12, air-cooled Twin-turbo diesel engine 560 kW (750 hp)
Range: 480 km (300 miles)

MECH COMBAT TEAM

"No way those Niners are going to get another trophy, man. Marino and the Dolphins will grab it next time - gotta lose one to win one!" Corporal Jankowicz tapped the M-16 magazine against his helmet then loaded it and racked the bolt.

"Right, that's what Larry Bird is telling the Celtics," Private Mackson ducked down as a spray of heavy automatic fire pelted against the walls of their position. The 1st Armored had been holding the Soviets off at Bayrueth for two days now ever since the Russians had poured across the border.

"Guess they don't like the Celtics either!" Jankowicz leaned above the shattered window frame and fired a quick burst down the street. Enemy infantry were hugging the buildings, getting ready to assault. An armoured troop carrier crawled around a distant corner and began firing. "Andrews! Get that BMP!"

Moments later, a Dragon round roared out of the 2nd floor and impacted right where the small turret met the hull of the enemy vehicle. A savage fireball exploded out of the stricken vehicle, flames and smoke billowing up.

Undeterred by the loss of their support, the enemy infantry began to fire and manoeuvre up the street. "Knock 'em back!" Jankowicz ordered, and the rest of the squad began firing short bursts. Mortar rounds began to land among the Soviets. Moments later, they began to withdraw, leaving dead and wounded behind.

"Anyone injured?" he yelled out.

"Just patching up Jones. Nothing serious." Andrews called down. "That was my last Dragon round Janko!"

That was serious, if any more tanks or assault vehicles approached they would have to let them get real close to use one of the lighter LAW shots. The ammo expenditure had been intense.

"Ok Andrews, go scrounge some. And get some rations while you're at it."

They would need to move soon. The enemy knew exactly where they were, and this building had taken a lot of damage. They would re-position and keep knocking the Ivans back. Old Ironsides would endure.

A mechanized infantry battalion contains four mechanized rifle companies and supporting weapons from the battalion HQ. These four companies form the basis of four mech combat teams. Each company is made up of a number of mech platoons, anti-tank platoons with M901 ITV anti-tank missile carriers, heavy mortar platoons with M106 mortar carriers, and scout sections from the battalion head-quarters, as well as a tank platoon from one of the brigade's armoured battalions.

Though not as hard hitting as the Armored Combat Team, the Mech Combat Team is ideally suited for holding and taking difficult terrain like woods and urban areas.

The fire support provided by their M901 ITV carriers, heavy mortars and tanks makes them capable of holding off most enemy forces when in defence.

On attack their M113 armoured personnel carriers allow them to advance into enemy contact, and dismount to fight. Supporting tanks and M901 ITV TOW missile carriers take care of any enemy armoured threat, while the M106 heavy mortars pound the positions of enemy infantry. Once the enemy is overcome, they can quickly remount their M113 armoured personnel carriers and continue their advance on to the next objective.

All this is not done in isolation. A Mech Combat Team can call on artillery, attack helicopters, strike aircraft, and other combat teams to support their operation, bringing the additional firepower provided by the brigade, division, and corps to the battle.

M113 MECH COMBAT TEAM

TEAM YANKEE

M113 MECH COMBAT TEAM HQ
TU103a

1x M16 rifle team, and
1x M113 (TU105)

1 POINT

• INFANTRY FORMATION • HQ TRANSPORT •

COURAGE 3+	SKILL 3+
MORALE 3+	ASSAULT 4+
RALLY 3+	COUNTERATTACK 3+

IS HIT ON	INFANTRY SAVE
4+	3+

TACTICAL	TERRAIN DASH	CROSS COUNTRY DASH	ROAD DASH	CROSS
8"/20CM	8"/20CM	12"/30CM	12"/30CM	AUTO

WEAPON	RANGE	ROF HALTED	MOVING	ANTI-TANK	FIRE-POWER	NOTES
M16 rifle team	12"/30CM	2	1	1	5+	

TEAM YANKEE

M113 MECH PLATOON
TU104

TEAM YANKEE

M113 MECH PLATOON
TU104

TEAM YANKEE

M113 MECH PLATOON
TU104

TEAM YANKEE

M1 ABRAMS TANK PLATOON
TU102a

OR

TEAM YANKEE

M60 PATTON TANK PLATOON
TU132

TEAM YANKEE

M106 HEAVY MORTAR PLATOON
TU108

TEAM YANKEE

M113 SCOUT SECTION
TU113

TEAM YANKEE

M901 ITV ANTI-TANK PLATOON
TU106

M113 MECH PLATOON

M113 MECH PLATOON

4x M249 SAW team with
   M72 LAW anti-tank
3x M47 Dragon missile team
4x M113 (TU105)   **6 POINTS**

3x M249 SAW team with
   M72 LAW anti-tank
2x M47 Dragon missile team
3x M113 (TU105)   **4 POINTS**

OPTIONS
• Add 1x M47 Dragon missile team for
  +1 point.

• INFANTRY UNIT • THERMAL IMAGING •

COURAGE 4+	SKILL 4+
MORALE 4+	ASSAULT 4+
RALLY 4+	COUNTERATTACK 4+

IS HIT ON	INFANTRY SAVE
4+	**3+**

TACTICAL	TERRAIN DASH	CROSS COUNTRY DASH	ROAD DASH	CROSS
8"/20cm	8"/20cm	12"/30cm	12"/30cm	AUTO

WEAPON	RANGE	ROF HALTED	ROF MOVING	ANTI-TANK	FIRE-POWER	NOTES
M249 SAW team	12"/30cm	3	2	1	5+	
or M72 LAW anti-tank	12"/30cm	1	1	12	5+	HEAT, Slow Firing
M47 Dragon missile	8"/20cm– 28"/70cm	1	-	18	3+	Assault 5, Guided, HEAT

The mech platoon is the latest in a long line of American armoured infantry units. Mounted in M113 armoured personnel carriers (APCs), the platoon is highly mobile, and well protected on the move. Once they dismount, the infantry have everything they need to fight on foot against any opposition. Each infantry squad is armed with the standard M16 rifle and the M249 SAW (Squad Automatic Weapon), a high rate-of-fire machine-gun in the same 5.56mm calibre. Two members of each squad have underslung M203 grenade launchers, giving them the firepower to tackle dug-in infantry as well as firing a useful buckshot round for close-in defence. Their anti-tank complement is made up of the short-range, disposable M72 LAW (Light Anti-tank Weapon) rocket launcher and the longer-ranged M47 Dragon anti-tank guided missile.

M113 TRANSPORT

DRAGON MOUNT: *A Mech Platoon* (TU104) *may remove M47 Dragon missile teams before the game, mounting an M47 Dragon missile on one of the Unit's M113 tracks for each team removed.*

The M113 armoured personnel carrier has served in the US Army since 1960, and with tens of thousands built, this versatile vehicle still has decades of service left in it. Designed to carry a squad of infantry into battle, safe from small-arms fire and artillery fragments under its revolutionary light-weight aluminium armour, the M113 is the classic modern infantry carrier.

Once the infantry have dismounted, the 'tracks' support them with long-range fire. For this role, they can mount the infantry squad's M47 Dragon beside the machine-gun. As improvised tank-killers, the tracks can manoeuvre onto the flanks of attacking tanks.

• TANK ATTACHMENT • AMPHIBIOUS • DRAGON MOUNT • PASSENGERS 3 • THERMAL IMAGING •

COURAGE 4+	SKILL 4+
MORALE 4+	ASSAULT 5+
REMOUNT 4+	COUNTERATTACK 5+

IS HIT ON 4+		
FRONT	SIDE	TOP
🚗 3	🚛 2	▬ 1

TACTICAL	TERRAIN DASH	CROSS COUNTRY DASH	ROAD DASH	CROSS
10"/25cm	16"/40cm	24"/60cm	32"/80cm	3+

WEAPON	RANGE	ROF HALTED	ROF MOVING	ANTI-TANK	FIRE-POWER	NOTES
.50 cal AA MG	20"/50cm	3	2	4	5+	
Optional M47 Dragon missile	8"/20cm– 28"/70cm	1	-	18	3+	Guided, HEAT

Crew: 2 - commander, driver
Weight: 12 tonnes
Length: 4.86m (16')
Width: 2.69m (8' 10")
Height: 1.83m (6')

Weapons: M2HB .50 cal MG
M47 Dragon anti-tank guided missile (Optional)
Armour: 38mm Aluminium
Speed: 68 km/h (42 mph)

M106 HEAVY MORTAR PLATOON

M106 HEAVY MORTAR PLATOON	
6x M106	**6 POINTS**
3x M106	**3 POINTS**

The M106 (107mm) self-propelled mortar mounts the M30 107mm (4.2") mortar on a turntable in the rear of the standard M113 APC. The M113 chassis allows the mortars to keep pace with the tank platoons, while protecting their crews against artillery splinters and small arms fire, ensuring immediate support when required.

• TANK UNIT • AMPHIBIOUS •

COURAGE 4+	SKILL 4+
MORALE 4+	ASSAULT 5+
REMOUNT 4+	COUNTERATTACK 5+

IS HIT ON 4+

FRONT	SIDE	TOP
3	2	0

TACTICAL	TERRAIN DASH	CROSS COUNTRY DASH	ROAD DASH	CROSS
10"/25CM	16"/40CM	24"/60CM	32"/80CM	3+

WEAPON	RANGE	ROF HALTED	ROF MOVING	ANTI-TANK	FIRE-POWER	NOTES
M30 107mm mortar	48"/120CM	ARTILLERY		2	4+	Smoke Bombardment
.50 cal AA MG	20"/50CM	3	2	4	5+	

M901 ITV ANTI-TANK PLATOON

M901 ITV ANTI-TANK PLATOON	
2x M901 ITV	**3 POINTS**

The M901 Improved TOW Vehicle (ITV) has a 'hammerhead' armoured turret housing two anti-tank guided missiles. With a range of 3000m, the Improved TOW missile (TOW stands for Tube-launched, Optically-tracked, Wire-guided) is the most widely used anti-tank guided missile in the West.

The hammerhead turret allows the M901 to sit behind cover with only the sights and missile tubes showing, ready to fire on advancing Soviet tanks. The TOW missile is quite capable of dealing with a Soviet main battle tank. Once it has fired, the M901 lowers its hammerhead launcher, and moves to another location where it reloads and repeats the performance.

• TANK UNIT •   • AMPHIBIOUS • HAMMERHEAD • THERMAL IMAGING •

COURAGE 4+	SKILL 4+
MORALE 4+	ASSAULT 5+
REMOUNT 4+	COUNTERATTACK 5+

IS HIT ON 4+

FRONT	SIDE	TOP
3	2	1

TACTICAL	TERRAIN DASH	CROSS COUNTRY DASH	ROAD DASH	CROSS
10"/25CM	16"/40CM	24"/60CM	32"/80CM	3+

WEAPON	RANGE	ROF HALTED	ROF MOVING	ANTI-TANK	FIRE-POWER	NOTES
Improved TOW missile	8"/20CM–48"/120CM	1	-	21	3+	Guided, HEAT
7.62mm AA MG	16"/40CM	3	3	2	6	

CAVALRY TROOP

Boiling dust clouds trailed behind the hard-revving Humvees as they sped towards Lt. Belgrove. He leaned into his binoculars, resting against the turret hatch rim of his M1 Abrams tank. His Cavalry Troop was positioned north-east of Hof, looking for the advanced elements of the Soviet 1st Guards Tank Army that had come pouring across the West German Border early on 4 August. The 2nd Cav had been on high alert waiting to see if the Bear was actually going to pull the trigger. The fish-tailing Hummers answered that. The M901's were hull down to his right, with just the launch units visible over the rise of the slope his tank rested on. This was going to be pure Cavalry action - hit and redeploy. Shoot from unexpected angles and then disappear. Slow and confuse the enemy, and allow time for the main forces to prepare further back.

Cobra gunships suddenly popped up in the distance, flying nap of the earth and spewing flares out behind them as angry missile contrails converged from several points towards them. They disappeared into another vale, then flashed into view before hammering overhead with the rotor wash flattening the vegetation around his tank and making the nearby trees thrash wildly.

Clicking his throat mike for the Troop net, he spoke firmly. "Wait for my mark. We need this first shot to put them on their heels." He switched to the internal comms and heard his driver, Carter, humming the Stones "Start me Up". He smiled, before instructing, "driver - two rounds and then back to point Alpha."

Movement caught his eye as the first enemy unit appeared. A 4-wheeled recon vehicle. It paused, then rolled down slope and out of sight. "Wait for the tracks" Blegrove reminded his gunner. The turret rotated slightly. A BMP nosed into sight, followed by several more. That was enough, time to engage. Activating the Troop net again, he gave the order: "All units - fire!"

ARMORED CAVALRY REGIMENT

The VII Corps first line of defence are the watchful scouts of the 2nd Armored Cavalry Regiment. Deployed along the VII Corps front they watch for the first signs of enemy movement. Once an enemy attack is underway they fight a series of delaying actions to hold and delay the enemy attack, buying time for the corps's divisions to deploy to their defensive positions. The regiment's preplanned ambush positions take full advantage of the firepower offered by its weapon systems.

Equipped with a mix of M1 Abrams main battle tanks, M113 APCs, M901 ITV anti-tank missile vehicles, and Cobra attack helicopters, the 2nd Armored Cavalry Regiment can hold its own against any likely Soviet thrust into its sector of northern Bavaria. They defeat Soviets scouts with ease and lay waste to following armoured forces, before slipping stealthily to their next ambush position.

THE BATTALION SCOUTS

Every commander needs a way of finding out where the enemy are and where they aren't. The divisional and corps commander have the cavalry for this role, but the battalion and company commander needs something more immediate.

That's where the scout platoon comes in. When setting up a defence, the battalion commander sends the scouts out in front to give warning of approaching enemy and to destroy their scouts. Once contact is made, they fall back to cover the flanks, watching for enemy infiltration. When the battalion returns to the attack, the scouts take the lead, seeking out enemy forces and either destroying them if they can, or holding them in place until the heavy units arrive to finish the job.

The scout platoon has three scout sections, each with one M113 scout track backed up by an M901 Improved Tow Vehicle (ITV). These sections spread out across the battalion front to achieve maximum coverage, with one or two sections in front of each of the forward combat teams.

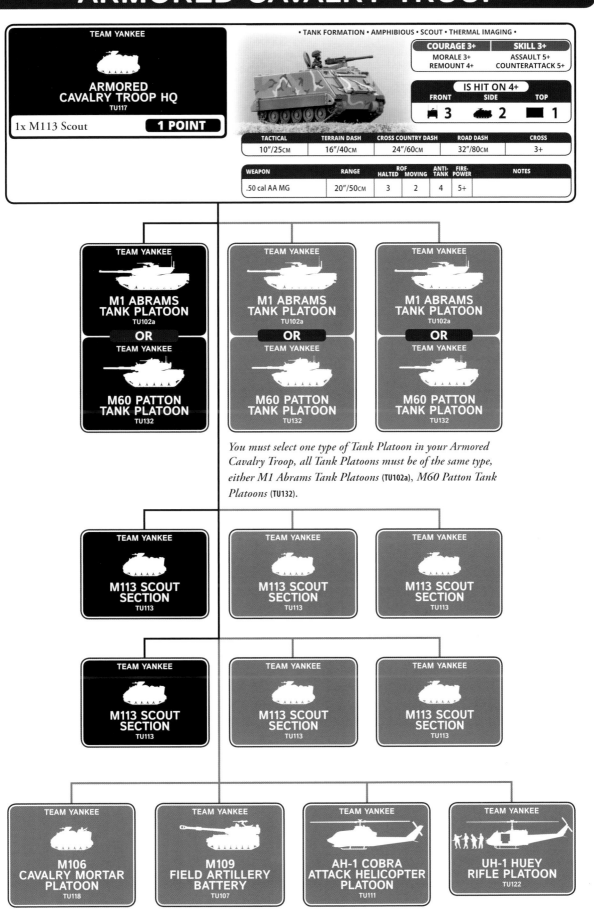

TEAM YANKEE
ARMORED CAVALRY TROOP

• TANK FORMATION • AMPHIBIOUS • SCOUT • THERMAL IMAGING •

TEAM YANKEE

ARMORED CAVALRY TROOP HQ
TU117

1x M113 Scout · **1 POINT**

COURAGE 3+	SKILL 3+
MORALE 3+	ASSAULT 5+
REMOUNT 4+	COUNTERATTACK 5+

IS HIT ON 4+

FRONT	SIDE	TOP
3	2	1

TACTICAL	TERRAIN DASH	CROSS COUNTRY DASH	ROAD DASH	CROSS
10"/25CM	16"/40CM	24"/60CM	32"/80CM	3+

WEAPON	RANGE	ROF HALTED	ROF MOVING	ANTI-TANK	FIRE-POWER	NOTES
.50 cal AA MG	20"/50CM	3	2	4	5+	

TEAM YANKEE
M1 ABRAMS TANK PLATOON
TU102a
OR
TEAM YANKEE
M60 PATTON TANK PLATOON
TU132

TEAM YANKEE
M1 ABRAMS TANK PLATOON
TU102a
OR
TEAM YANKEE
M60 PATTON TANK PLATOON
TU132

TEAM YANKEE
M1 ABRAMS TANK PLATOON
TU102a
OR
TEAM YANKEE
M60 PATTON TANK PLATOON
TU132

You must select one type of Tank Platoon in your Armored Cavalry Troop, all Tank Platoons must be of the same type, either M1 Abrams Tank Platoons (TU102a), M60 Patton Tank Platoons (TU132).

TEAM YANKEE
M113 SCOUT SECTION
TU113

TEAM YANKEE
M113 SCOUT SECTION
TU113

TEAM YANKEE
M113 SCOUT SECTION
TU113

TEAM YANKEE
M113 SCOUT SECTION
TU113

TEAM YANKEE
M113 SCOUT SECTION
TU113

TEAM YANKEE
M113 SCOUT SECTION
TU113

TEAM YANKEE
M106 CAVALRY MORTAR PLATOON
TU118

TEAM YANKEE
M109 FIELD ARTILLERY BATTERY
TU107

TEAM YANKEE
AH-1 COBRA ATTACK HELICOPTER PLATOON
TU111

TEAM YANKEE
UH-1 HUEY RIFLE PLATOON
TU122

M113 SCOUT SECTION

M113 SCOUT SECTION

1x M113 Scout
1x M901 ITV

2 POINTS

• TANK UNIT • AMPHIBIOUS •   • SCOUT • SPEARHEAD • THERMAL IMAGING •

COURAGE 4+	SKILL 4+
MORALE 4+	ASSAULT 6
REMOUNT 4+	COUNTERATTACK -

IS HIT ON 4+

FRONT	SIDE	TOP
3	2	1

TACTICAL	TERRAIN DASH	CROSS COUNTRY DASH	ROAD DASH	CROSS
10"/25CM	16"/40CM	24"/60CM	32"/80CM	3+

WEAPON	RANGE	HALTED	MOVING	ANTI-TANK	FIRE-POWER	NOTES
M113 Scout with .50 cal MG	20"/50CM	3	2	4	5+	
M901 ITV with 7.62mm AA MG	16"/40CM	3	3	2	6	
M901 ITV with Improved TOW missile	8"/20CM–48"/120CM	1	-	21	3+	Guided, HEAT, Hammerhead

The versatile M113 armoured personnel carrier is the basis for both of the scout section's vehicles. The lead vehicle is a basic model M113 fitted with a special cupola mounting the standard M2HB .50 cal machine-gun. While tall for a scout vehicle, the M113 is reliable and well protected, and its armament is more than enough to deal with opposing scouting forces.

The M113 is backed up by a hard-hitting M901 ITV. Both vehicles carry a pair of scouts. These allow the tracks to remain concealed while the scouts sneak to the edge of cover to observe the enemy, significantly increasing their stealthiness.

SCOUT TACTICS

The combination of an M113 track and an M901 ITV gives the scout section a lot of versatility. The scouts advance cautiously, with the M113 moving forward covered by the M901 ITV. If the M113 comes under fire, the M901 ITV responds immediately as the M113 dashes for cover.

If the M113 reaches the next piece of cover without coming under fire, it pauses to observe the surrounding terrain.

Once it is certain that there are no enemy to hand, the M901 ITV moves up to join it, then the M113 advances to the next piece of cover and the process repeats.

This careful process allows the scouts to work their way forward without being spotted by the enemy. The combat teams following the scouts can then move forward, confident in the knowledge that they won't reveal their presence until they are ready to strike.

M106 CAVALRY MORTAR PLATOON

M106 CAVALRY MORTAR PLATOON

3x M106

3 POINTS

• TANK UNIT • AMPHIBIOUS •

COURAGE 4+	SKILL 4+
MORALE 4+	ASSAULT 5+
REMOUNT 4+	COUNTERATTACK 5+

IS HIT ON 4+

FRONT	SIDE	TOP
3	2	0

TACTICAL	TERRAIN DASH	CROSS COUNTRY DASH	ROAD DASH	CROSS
10"/25CM	16"/40CM	24"/60CM	32"/80CM	3+

WEAPON	RANGE	ROF HALTED	MOVING	ANTI-TANK	FIRE-POWER	NOTES
M30 107mm mortar	48"/120CM	ARTILLERY		2	4+	Smoke Bombardment
.50 cal AA MG	20"/50CM	3	2	4	5+	

The M106 (107mm) self-propelled mortar mounts the M30 107mm (4.2") mortar on a turntable in the rear of the standard M113 personnel carrier. The M113 chassis allows the mortars to keep pace with the tank platoons, while protecting their crews against artillery splinters and small arms fire, ensuring immediate support when required.

LIGHT DIVISION RECONNAISSANCE SQUADRON

The US divisions organised under the light division structure, such as the 82nd Airborne, had one reconnaissance squadron with one light cavalry troop mounted in wheeled vehicles. These had initially been jeeps, but by 1985 had been replaced by the new High Mobility Multipurpose Wheeled Vehicle (HMMWV), 'Humvee' or 'Hummer' as it quickly became known to the troops.

Each troop had three variants of the HMMWV armaments carrier available, 14 with .50 cal machine-guns or 40mm Mk 19 grenade launchers, and eight mounting Improved TOW anti-tank missiles. A light cavalry troop is organised into six scout sections of four HMMWV vehicles, one armed with a M2 .50 cal machine-gun, one with a 40mm Mk19 grenade launcher and one or two with ITOW launchers.

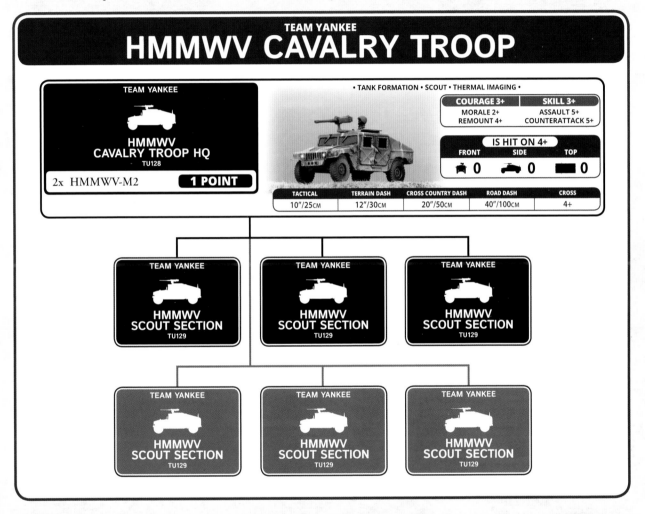

TEAM YANKEE
HMMWV CAVALRY TROOP

TEAM YANKEE

HMMWV CAVALRY TROOP HQ
TU128

2x HMMWV-M2 — **1 POINT**

• TANK FORMATION • SCOUT • THERMAL IMAGING •

COURAGE 3+	SKILL 3+
MORALE 2+	ASSAULT 5+
REMOUNT 4+	COUNTERATTACK 5+

IS HIT ON 4+

FRONT	SIDE	TOP
0	0	0

TACTICAL	TERRAIN DASH	CROSS COUNTRY DASH	ROAD DASH	CROSS
10"/25CM	12"/30CM	20"/50CM	40"/100CM	4+

TEAM YANKEE
HMMWV SCOUT SECTION
TU129

TEAM YANKEE
HMMWV SCOUT SECTION
TU129

TEAM YANKEE
HMMWV SCOUT SECTION
TU129

TEAM YANKEE
HMMWV SCOUT SECTION
TU129

TEAM YANKEE
HMMWV SCOUT SECTION
TU129

TEAM YANKEE
HMMWV SCOUT SECTION
TU129

TEAM YANKEE
HMMWV SCOUT SECTION

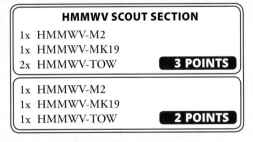

HMMWV SCOUT SECTION

1x HMMWV-M2
1x HMMWV-MK19
2x HMMWV-TOW — **3 POINTS**

1x HMMWV-M2
1x HMMWV-MK19
1x HMMWV-TOW — **2 POINTS**

The excellent mobility of the HMMWV vehicle proved them ideal scouts. Much like their armoured brothers, the HMMWV scouts advance in bounds. The HMMWV-M2 or HMMWV-Mk19 cautiously advance to the next observation position, all the while being covered by the remaining HMMWVs.

• TANK UNIT • SCOUT • SPEARHEAD • THERMAL IMAGING •

COURAGE 4+	SKILL 4+
MORALE 3+	ASSAULT -
REMOUNT 4+	COUNTERATTACK -

IS HIT ON 4+

FRONT	SIDE	TOP
0	0	0

TACTICAL	TERRAIN DASH	CROSS COUNTRY DASH	ROAD DASH	CROSS
10"/25CM	12"/30CM	20"/50CM	40"/100CM	4+

WEAPON	RANGE	ROF HALTED	ROF MOVING	ANTI-TANK	FIRE-POWER	NOTES
HMMWV-M2 with .50 cal AA MG	20"/50CM	3	2	4	5+	
HMMWV-MK19 with 40mm grenade launcher	16"/40CM	5	4	4	6	
HMMWV-TOW with Improved TOW missile	8"/20CM– 48"/120CM	1	-	21	3+	Guided, HEAT

82ND AIRBORNE

The 82nd Airborne Division has a long and proud history dating back to its formation during the First World War as the 82nd Division in 1917. It was during this period a competition was held to find the division's nickname in Atlanta, Georgia. 'All American' was the result, reflecting the division's composition of members from all 48 states. It sailed to France and took part in the St. Mihiel and Meuse-Argonne offensives in 1918. After the war it was demobilised and was listed as a reserve division.

When the United States entered WWII the 82nd Division was raised again in February 1942. In August 1942 the 82nd Division became the United States first airborne division and was made up of glider-borne and parachute infantry. The division's first airborne operations occurred during the invasion of Sicily on 9 July 1943, then again at Salerno on the Italian mainland on 13 September 1943. The division then took part in the in the landings in the Normandy invasion, making airborne landings on 6 June 1944 behind German positions before the seaborne landings. They went on to fight in Operation Market Garden in the Netherlands, during the Battle of the Bulge and the conquest of Germany.

After WWII the division was not demobilized, and instead moved to a permanent home at Fort Bragg, North Carolina. The division was eventually designated a permanent division in 1948. The division spent most of the 1950s in hard training in a variety of environments and didn't take part in the Korean War as they were held back as a strategic reserve in case of Soviet aggression. During the 1960s and 1970s they served in the Dominican Republic, Vietnam, and deployed in South Korea.

In the 1980s, the 82nd 'All American' Airborne Division formed the nucleus of the newly created Rapid Deployment Forces (RDF), a mobile force permanently in a high state of readiness. On 25 October 1983, elements of the 82nd Airborne took part in the US intervention on the Caribbean island of Grenada. They secured Point Salinas Airport following an airborne assault by the 1st and 2nd Ranger Battalions. In all six infantry battalions of the 82nd took part in the Grenada operation. The 82nd advanced from the airhead at Salinas to weed out Cuban and Grenadian soldiers until the fighting ended in early November. The operation identified several areas to improve on the new Rapid Deployment Forces doctrine. Among these were unsuitable uniforms for the tropical environment, and communication issues between the Army ground forces, Navy, and Air Force elements. However, the operation proved the division's ability to act as a rapid deployment force.

When war broke out on 4 August 1985, followed by the rapid advance across West Germany by Warsaw Pact forces in the following days, the Joint Chiefs of Staff were prompted to release the 82nd Airborne Division to the US European Command where it was assigned to the VII Corps to take part in the offensive into East Germany.

82nd Airborne Division was organised as a light infantry division. The primary characteristics of a light infantry division are its mission flexibility, rapid deployment, and combat readiness at 100 percent strength.

INFANTRY COMBAT TEAM

The clatter of rotor blades was constant. Swarms of Huey transports were inbound, landing, disgorging and taking off to get another load. The 82nd Airborne had leaped across the Saale River as part of the rolling counter-attack against Soviet forces. The bridgehead was still fragile, but getting stronger every minute. Sergeant Golton led his squad into the tree line as the first wavering rocket rounds began to impact on the landing zone, throwing up dense blast clouds that whirled into strange contortions from all the competing drafts.

"Igor will be closing in fast! Jacobs - get a sight line down that path. Use the LAW's on any vehicles that come around the bend. Chaz! Contact the —"

A burst of fire sent every trooper burrowing for cover, as the first BRDM-2 recon vehicle came bouncing up the path, spraying MG fire wildly. Jacobs leaned out from behind cover and fired. The LAW round bored through the glacis and caused havoc as the BRDM crashed off the path before rolling over. Private Levitz popped a grenade through the hatch as insurance.

Assault rifle rounds began tearing through their position, so the squad returned fire. Golton grabbed another LAW from Corporal Levitz and slung it over towards Jacobs. "There'll be more! Get ready!"

With a rush of down wash, and heavy thumping, a pair of Cobras hovered overhead. One fired an electric hose of 20mm rounds on to a target deeper in the woods, while the other launched TOW missiles at a distant enemy. They peeled away, just as a Hummer with an ungainly looking TOW launcher mounted on top came up behind them.

Lt. Polson leaned out from the passenger door, "Engineers have started on the bridge! We're moving forward!" Columns of boiling black smoke were visible above the trees tops ahead as Golton waved his squad up. "Just another day for the Airborne!" he called out as they pushed deeper into the trees.

The main combat power of a light infantry division, like the 82nd Airborne Division, comes from its nine rifle battalions. Each battalion has three rifle companies as well as scout, mortar, anti-armour, and support platoons. Each company contains three rifle platoons and various company head-quarters weapons that can be allocated out as required for the mission.

Further supporting elements are also available from the division's artillery and aviation brigades, as well as the divisional level air defence battalion, and in the case of the 82nd Airborne Division, it's tank battalion (3rd Battalion, 73rd Armored Regiment) with its air transportable M551 Sheridan air assault vehicles.

The 82nd Aviation Brigade provides Cobra attack helicopters for tank hunting in both defensive and offensive operations. The brigade's UH-1 Huey transport helicopters are available for air assault operations. These allow the riflemen to land behind enemy lines and quickly seize vital objectives.

UH-1 HUEY INFANTRY COMBAT TEAM

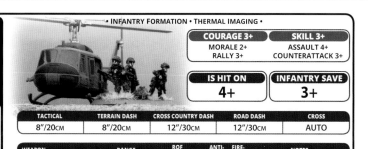
• INFANTRY FORMATION • THERMAL IMAGING •

TEAM YANKEE

UH-1 HUEY INFANTRY COMBAT TEAM HQ
TU121

| 1x M16 rifle team | **1 POINT** |

The Formation Commander rides with one of the UH-1 Huey Rifle Platoons (TU122).

COURAGE 3+	SKILL 3+
MORALE 2+	ASSAULT 4+
RALLY 3+	COUNTERATTACK 3+

IS HIT ON	INFANTRY SAVE
4+	**3+**

TACTICAL	TERRAIN DASH	CROSS COUNTRY DASH	ROAD DASH	CROSS
8"/20CM	8"/20CM	12"/30CM	12"/30CM	AUTO

WEAPON	RANGE	ROF HALTED	ROF MOVING	ANTI-TANK	FIRE-POWER	NOTES
M16 rifle team	12"/30CM	2	1	1	5+	

TEAM YANKEE

UH-1 HUEY RIFLE PLATOON
TU122

TEAM YANKEE

UH-1 HUEY RIFLE PLATOON
TU122

TEAM YANKEE

M551 SHERIDAN TANK PLATOON
TU127

TEAM YANKEE

M551 SHERIDAN TANK PLATOON
TU127

TEAM YANKEE

UH-1 HUEY RIFLE PLATOON
TU122

TEAM YANKEE

HMMWV SCOUT SECTION
TU129

TEAM YANKEE

HMMWV-TOW ANTI-TANK PLATOON
TU126

UH-1 HUEY RIFLE PLATOON

UH-1 HUEY RIFLE PLATOON

7x M249 SAW team with
   M72 LAW anti-tank
1x M47 Dragon missile team
3x UH-1 Huey (TU123)   **8 POINTS**

5x M249 SAW team with
   M72 LAW anti-tank
1x M47 Dragon missile team
2x UH-1 Huey (TU123)   **6 POINTS**

OPTIONS

- Add 1x M47 Dragon missile team for +1 point.
- Add up to 2x M60 GPMG teams for +1 point each.
- Add 1x M224 60mm mortar team for +1 point.
- Add 1x UH-1 Huey (TU123) at no cost.

• INFANTRY UNIT • THERMAL IMAGING •

COURAGE 4+	SKILL 4+
MORALE 3+	ASSAULT 4+
RALLY 4+	COUNTERATTACK 4+

IS HIT ON	INFANTRY SAVE
4+	**3+**

TACTICAL	TERRAIN DASH	CROSS COUNTRY DASH	ROAD DASH	CROSS
8"/20CM	8"/20CM	12"/30CM	12"/30CM	AUTO

WEAPON	RANGE	ROF HALTED	ROF MOVING	ANTI-TANK	FIRE-POWER	NOTES
M249 SAW team or M72 LAW anti-tank	12"/30CM 12"/30CM	3 1	2 1	1 12	5+ 5+	 HEAT, Slow Firing
M47 Dragon missile	8"/20CM– 28"/70CM	1	-	18	3+	Assault 5, Guided, HEAT
M60 GPMG	16"/40CM	5	2	2	6	Assault 5
M224 60mm mortar	32"/80CM	1	1	1	4+	Assault 5, Overhead Fire, Slow Firing

The rifle platoons of the 82nd Airborne Division are bigger than the mech platoons of the heavy divisions. Each has three large rifle squads (9 men each), a headquarters (5 men), and a weapons squad (7 men). The rifle squads are divided into two fire teams each with a M249 squad automatic weapon (SAW) and a M203 grenade launcher in addition to M16A1 assault rifles and LAW anti-tank weapons.

The weapons squad provides further firepower with a pair of M60 general purpose machine-guns (GPMG). Dragon anti-tank missiles teams are attached from the battalion anti-armour platoon.

For mobility UH-1 Huey helicopter are attached from the 82nd Aviation Brigade for air assault capabilities.

UH-1 HUEY TRANSPORT HELICOPTER

DOOR GUNS: UH-1 Huey helicopters have door mounted M60 machine-guns to cover their passengers when they dismount and mount during air assault missions. Helicopters are vulnerable to enemy ground fire when coming into the landing zone, so unload and load quickly, and tend not to waste precious ammunition and time on other targets.

Unlike other Helicopters, UH-1 Huey's with Door Guns can Shoot while Landed. Door Guns can only Shoot in the turn that they Land.

• HELICOPTER AIRCRAFT ATTACHMENT • PASSENGERS 3 •

COURAGE 4+	SKILL 4+
MORALE 3+	

IS HIT ON	AIRCRAFT SAVE
4+	**5+**

TACTICAL	TERRAIN DASH	CROSS COUNTRY DASH	ROAD DASH	CROSS
UNLIMITED				AUTO

WEAPON	RANGE	ROF HALTED	ROF MOVING	ANTI-TANK	FIRE-POWER	NOTES
Door M60 MGs	16"/40CM	4	4	2	6	Door Guns

The UH-1H Huey utility helicopters of the 82nd Aviation Brigade provide the riflemen of the 82nd Airborne Division with airlift capability for quick in-theatre redeployment, and for air assault combat operations for insertion into the enemy's rear area.

Each Huey is fitted with a pair of M60 machine-guns mounted at the side doors to give covering fire during landing and unloading or loading of passengers. The M60 door guns are crewed by a dedicated door gunner and the crew chief.

Crew: 2-4 - pilot, co-pilot, crew chief, door gunner
Empty Weight: 2.36 tonnes (5,215 lb)
Length: 17.40m (57' 1")
Width: 2.62m (8' 7")
Height: 4.39m (14' 5')
Weapons: 2 × 7.62 mm M60 MG

Cruise Speed: 201 km/h (125 mph; 109 kn)
Capacity: 1,760 kg (3,880 lb) including 14 troops, or 6 stretchers, or equivalent cargo
Range: 507 km (315 miles)
Service ceiling: 5,910m (19,390 feet)

TEAM YANKEE
HMMWV-TOW ANTI-TANK PLATOON

HMMWV-TOW ANTI-TANK PLATOON	
4x HMMWV-TOW	**4 POINTS**
2x HMMWV-TOW	**2 POINTS**

The anti-armor platoon of a rifle battalion is equipped with Improved TOW anti-tank guided missiles. For added mobility these have been mounted on the new HMMWV weapons carrier. The TOW can be fired easily from the weapons position next to the driver, making it simple for the TOW team to reposition after firing.

• TANK UNIT • SCOUT • THERMAL IMAGING •

COURAGE 4+	SKILL 4+
MORALE 3+	ASSAULT 6
REMOUNT 4+	COUNTERATTACK 6

IS HIT ON 4+		
FRONT	SIDE	TOP
0	0	0

TACTICAL	TERRAIN DASH	CROSS COUNTRY DASH	ROAD DASH	CROSS
10"/25CM	12"/30CM	20"/50CM	40"/100CM	4+

WEAPON	RANGE	ROF HALTED	ROF MOVING	ANTI-TANK	FIRE-POWER	NOTES
Improved TOW missile	8"/20CM–48"/120CM	1	-	21	3+	Guided, HEAT

TEAM YANKEE
M551 SHERIDAN TANK PLATOON

M551 SHERIDAN TANK PLATOON	
5x M551 Sheridan	**10 POINTS**
4x M551 Sheridan	**8 POINTS**
3x M551 Sheridan	**6 POINTS**
2x M551 Sheridan	**4 POINTS**

The M551 Sheridan Armored Reconnaissance/ Airborne Assault Vehicle, or ARAAV, is fitted with the M81 dual-purpose gun/missile launcher. It can fire conventional HEAT anti-tank ammunition for shorter range targets, or the MGM51 Shillelagh (pronounced shil-lay-lee) anti-tank guided missile, which was more effective at longer ranges.

In 1978 most Sheridans were phased out of service. However, the 82nd Airborne Division decided to keep the air transportable Sheridan airborne assault vehicle. These were upgraded with improved suspension.

During air assault missions the Sheridan could be parachuted, or delivered in a Low Altitude Parachute Extraction System (LAPES) drop from the back of a heavy transport aircraft.

• TANK UNIT • AMPHIBIOUS • INFRA-RED (IR) •

COURAGE 4+	SKILL 4+
MORALE 3+	ASSAULT 4+
REMOUNT 4+	COUNTERATTACK 4+

IS HIT ON 4+		
FRONT	SIDE	TOP
4	2	1

TACTICAL	TERRAIN DASH	CROSS COUNTRY DASH	ROAD DASH	CROSS
10"/25CM	16"/40CM	28"/70CM	32"/80CM	3+

WEAPON	RANGE	ROF HALTED	ROF MOVING	ANTI-TANK	FIRE-POWER	NOTES
M81 152mm gun	16"/40CM	1	1	21	1+	Brutal, HEAT, Stabiliser
or MGM51 Shillelagh missile	16"/40CM–48"/120CM	1	-	22	3+	Guided, HEAT
.50 cal AA MG	20"/50CM	3	2	4	5+	
7.62mm MG	16"/40CM	1	1	2	6	

Crew:	4 - commander, gunner, loader, driver	Armour:	Aluminum alloy (protection against 20mm AP)
Weight:	15.2 tonnes	Speed:	70 km/h (43 mph)
Length:	6.3m (20'7")	Engine:	Detroit Diesel 6V53T,
Width:	2.8m (9'1")		6 cylinder, turbocharged diesel
Height:	2.3m (7'6")		220 kW (300 hp)
Weapons:	M81E1 152 mm gun/launcher M2 .50 cal MG M219 7.62mm MG	Range:	560 km (348 miles)

ARMY SUPPORT

M48 CHAPARRAL SAM PLATOON

M48 CHAPARRAL SAM PLATOON	
4x M48 Chaparral	**8 POINTS**
2x M48 Chaparral	**4 POINTS**

• UNARMOURED TANK UNIT • INFRA-RED (IR) •

COURAGE 4+	SKILL 4+
MORALE 4+	ASSAULT -
RALLY 4+	COUNTERATTACK -

IS HIT ON	TANK SAVE
4+	**5+**

TACTICAL	TERRAIN DASH	CROSS COUNTRY DASH	ROAD DASH	CROSS
10"/25CM	14"/35CM	20"/50CM	28"/70CM	3+

WEAPON	RANGE	ROF HALTED	ROF MOVING	ANTI-TANK	FIRE-POWER	NOTES
MIM-72 Sidewinder AA Missile	72"/180CM	2	-	-	3+	Guided AA

The M48 Chaparral is a tried and tested surface-to-air missile (SAM) weapons system that first entered service with the US Army in 1969. This SAM system fires MIM-72G Chaparral missiles (based on the AIM-9 Sidewinder air-to-air missile) which use an infra-red seeker to lock on to the hot exhaust of an aircraft. The system is fired manually by the operator visually tracking the target, aiming the missile in the general direction, and waiting for the missile seekers to lock on to the target.

M247 SERGEANT YORK AA PLATOON

M247 SERGEANT YORK AA PLATOON	
4x M247 Sergeant York	**8 POINTS**
2x M247 Sergeant York	**4 POINTS**

• TANK UNIT • INFRA-RED (IR) •

COURAGE 4+	SKILL 4+
MORALE 4+	ASSAULT 5+
REMOUNT 4+	COUNTERATTACK 5+

IS HIT ON 4+		
FRONT	SIDE	TOP
4	3	1

TACTICAL	TERRAIN DASH	CROSS COUNTRY DASH	ROAD DASH	CROSS
10"/25CM	14"/35CM	20"/50CM	24"/60CM	3+

WEAPON	RANGE	ROF HALTED	ROF MOVING	ANTI-TANK	FIRE-POWER	NOTES
Twin 40mm AA gun	24"/60CM	5	4	7	4+	Dedicated AA, Radar

M247 Sergeant York came out of the DIVAD (DIVision Air Defense) programme to find a replacement for the M163 VADS and went into production in 1981.

Crew:	4 - commander, gunner, driver	Weapons:	2x Bofors 40 mm L/70
Weight:	49.35 tonnes (54.4 ton)		anti-aircraft guns
Length:	7.67m (25'2") (gun forward)	Engine:	Continental AVDS-1790-2D
	6.42m (21'0.75") (hull)		diesel
Width:	3.63m (11' 11")		560 kw (750 hp)
Height:	3.42m (11' 2.5")	Speed:	48 km/h (30 mph)

The M247 is fitted with fully-stabilized twin 40mm Bofors anti-aircraft guns and with a search and track radar designed to track aircraft out to a range of 40km. The Sergeant York is also fitted with a laser-rangefinder and digital fire control system. This was all housed in a new turret mounted on the hull of a M48A5 Patton medium tank.

Due to some development problems only 50 vehicles had been produced by 1985.

M163 VADS AA PLATOON

M163 VADS AA PLATOON	
4x M163 VADS	**6 POINTS**
2x M163 VADS	**3 POINTS**

The M163 Vulcan Air Defence System (VADS) is the US Army's main anti-air-artillery system. The M168 20mm Gatling gun is a modification of the M61 six-barrelled Vulcan cannon used by most modern US jet fighter. With a cyclic rate of fire of 3000 rpm, anything hit by the M168 stays hit.

The M163 is a simple system, relying on the gunner's eyesight to locate a target. However, once located, the ranging radar adjusts the sights to ensure a high probability of a hit.

• TANK UNIT • AMPHIBIOUS •

COURAGE 4+		SKILL 4+	
MORALE 4+		ASSAULT 5+	
REMOUNT 4+		COUNTERATTACK 5+	

IS HIT ON 4+

FRONT	SIDE	TOP
🛡 3	🚜 2	▬ 0

TACTICAL	TERRAIN DASH	CROSS COUNTRY DASH	ROAD DASH	CROSS
10"/25CM	16"/40CM	24"/60CM	32"/80CM	3+

WEAPON	RANGE	ROF HALTED	MOVING	ANTI-TANK	FIRE-POWER	NOTES
M168 20mm Vulcan Gatling AA gun	20"/50CM	7	4	6	5+	Dedicated AA, Radar

Crew: 4 - commander, gunner, loader, driver
Weight: 12.5 tonnes
Length: 4.86m (16')
Width: 2.69m (8' 10")
Height: 2.9m (9' 7")

Weapons: M168 20mm Vulcan Gatling gun
Armour: 38mm Aluminium
Speed: 68 km/h (42 mph)
Engine: GM 6V53 158 kW (212 hp) diesel

The guns of the M109 artillery pieces from the 17th Field Artillery were finally quiet. Repeated fire missions in support of the 3rd Infantry near Bamburg had exhausted the ready ammunition supplies. The gun crews were currently engaged in hauling crates of 155mm rounds for resupply, ear protectors slung round their necks and stripped to the waist. Captain Felder checked off the supply forms presented by his quartermaster, where would the army be without paperwork? One of the Chaparral AA vehicles suddenly rotated its ungainly turret, a shrieking roar accompanied by a choking cloud of smoke announced the launch of a missile from the turret rack.

Felder sprinted for the nearest trench, piling in with several others.

"Air or choppers?" he shouted. Blank looks from hunkered down heads. He peered over the trench lip and spotted a Soviet Hind helicopter lifting up above the tree line to the north-east. Two soldiers carrying a Stinger missile knelt down next to one of the M109s. Before they could even shoulder the weapon a whirlwind of cannon fire cut them down. The Chaparral exploded as an ATGM missile ploughed into it from another direction. The Hinds had come in numbers and were encircling them.

Tapping one of the men in the trench, he shouted "With me!" and sprinted towards the dropped Stinger, trusting that he was being followed. He picked up the missile and settled it on his shoulder, a hand tapped his shoulder and pointed towards the nearest target.

Before he had even uncaged the launcher, a bass roar erupted nearby. A stream of 40mm fire licked out to caress the Hind which instantly shook as debris, bodies, and parts of the fuselage showered out from it, before it began spiralling down and detonated in the forest. One of the new Sergeant York tracks rolled into view and swung its massive turret, equipped with twin 40mm cannons, in search of new targets.

TEAM YANKEE
HMMWV SAM PLATOON

HMMWV SAM PLATOON	
4x HMMWV Stinger	**4 POINTS**
2x HMMWV Stinger	**2 POINTS**

Not all Stinger teams have moved to the tracked anti-aircraft platoons. Some have swapped their jeeps for the more mobile HMMWV.

The highly manoeuvrable HMMWV weapons carrier allows the Stinger Man-portable air-defence systems (MANPADS) teams to keep pace with any combat team they are supporting.

• TANK UNIT •

COURAGE 4+	SKILL 4+
MORALE 4+	ASSAULT 5+
REMOUNT 4+	COUNTERATTACK 5+

IS HIT ON 4+		
FRONT	SIDE	TOP
0	0	0

TACTICAL	TERRAIN DASH	CROSS COUNTRY DASH	ROAD DASH	CROSS
10"/25CM	12"/30CM	20"/50CM	40"/100CM	4+

WEAPON	RANGE	ROF HALTED	MOVING	ANTI-TANK	FIRE-POWER	NOTES
Stinger AA missile	48"/120CM	2	-	-	4+	*Guided AA*

THE STINGER MISSILE

The FIM-92 Stinger anti-aircraft missile is a modern replacement for the older FIM-43 Redeye. The Stinger is slightly heavier, but far more deadly. It's missile is significantly faster, and with the new POST (Passive Optical Seeker Technique) upgrade, far less likely to be distracted by enemy countermeasures like flares. Most importantly though, its tracker is sensitive enough to be able to engage aircraft from any angle, unlike the older missile that could only be fired at the hot exhaust of a retreating aircraft. The arrival of the Stinger missile has made the airspace over the front lines far more dangerous for Soviet aircraft and helicopters.

M109 FIELD ARTILLERY BATTERY

M109 FIELD ARTILLERY BATTERY

| 6x M109 | **14 POINTS** |
| 3x M109 | **7 POINTS** |

OPTIONS

- Arm all M109 with Bomblets for +1 point.
- Arm all M109 with Minelets for +1 point.
- Arm all M109 with Laser-Guided Projectiles for +1 point each.

The excellence of the M109 self-propelled howitzer is evidenced by the fact that it is used by every Western army on NATO's Central Front apart from the French. The M185 155mm howitzer fires a wide variety of ammunition, including conventional high explosive, DPICM (Dual-Purpose Improved Conventional Munitions) bomblets, scatterable minelets, and Copperhead laser-guided projectiles out to a range of 18 km (11 miles).

• TANK UNIT • BOMBLETS • LASER-GUIDED PROJECTILES • MINELETS •

COURAGE 4+	SKILL 4+
MORALE 4+	ASSAULT 5+
REMOUNT 4+	COUNTERATTACK 5+

IS HIT ON 4+

FRONT	SIDE	TOP
2	2	1

TACTICAL	TERRAIN DASH	CROSS COUNTRY DASH	ROAD DASH	CROSS
10"/25CM	16"/40CM	24"/60CM	28"/70CM	3+

WEAPON	RANGE	ROF HALTED	ROF MOVING	ANTI-TANK	FIRE-POWER	NOTES
M185 155mm howitzer	96"/240CM	ARTILLERY		4	2+	Smoke Bombardment
or Direct fire	36"/90CM	1	1	15	1+	Brutal, Slow Firing, Smoke
.50 cal AA MG	20"/50CM	3	2	4	5+	

Crew: 6 – commander, 2x gunner, 2x loader, driver
Weight: 25 tonnes
Length: 9.1m (30')
Width: 3.15m (10' 4")
Height: 3.25m (10' 8")

Weapons: M185 155mm howitzer M2 HB .50 cal MG
Armour: 20mm
Speed: 54 km/h (34 mph)
Engine: 8V71T diesel 336 kW (450 hp)
Range: 350 km (215 miles)

M113 FIST

M113 FIST

| 1x M113 FIST | **1 POINT** |

You must field:

- *a Team Yankee M109 Field Artillery Battery* (TU107), *or*
- *a Team Yankee M106 Heavy Mortar Platoon* (TU108)

before you may field a Team Yankee M113 FIST.

A Fire Support Team is responsible for coordinating all of a company's supporting fires from artillery and aircraft.

• INDEPENDENT TANK UNIT • AMPHIBIOUS • OBSERVER • SCOUT • THERMAL IMAGING •

COURAGE 4+	SKILL 4+
MORALE 4+	ASSAULT 5+
REMOUNT 4+	COUNTERATTACK 5+

IS HIT ON 4+

FRONT	SIDE	TOP
3	2	1

TACTICAL	TERRAIN DASH	CROSS COUNTRY DASH	ROAD DASH	CROSS
10"/25CM	16"/40CM	24"/60CM	32"/80CM	3+

WEAPON	RANGE	ROF HALTED	ROF MOVING	ANTI-TANK	FIRE-POWER	NOTES
.50 cal AA MG	20"/50CM	3	2	4	5+	

TEAM YANKEE
A-10 WARTHOG FIGHTER FLIGHT

A-10 WARTHOG FIGHTER FLIGHT	
4x A-10 Warthog	**20 POINTS**
2x A-10 Warthog	**10 POINTS**

Although its official designation is the Thunderbolt II, the rather odd-looking A-10 is commonly, if unflatteringly, known as the 'Warthog'. The A-10 is built around a massive 30mm GAU-8/A Avenger seven-barrelled Gatling gun that fires depleted uranium rounds, and in its tank-busting role, carries TV-guided Maverick missiles. On top of that, its armoured cockpit and high-mounted engines give it outstanding resilience when hit by enemy fire.

• STRIKE AIRCRAFT UNIT •

COURAGE 4+	SKILL 4+
MORALE 4+	

IS HIT ON	AIRCRAFT SAVE
4+	**3+**

TACTICAL	TERRAIN DASH	CROSS COUNTRY DASH	ROAD DASH	CROSS
UNLIMITED				AUTO

WEAPON	RANGE	ROF HALTED	ROF MOVING	ANTI-TANK	FIRE-POWER	NOTES
GAU-8/A 30mm Gatling gun	8"/20CM	-	4	11	5+	Anti-helicopter
Maverick missile	8"/20CM–36"/90CM	-	1	27	2+	Brutal, Guided, HEAT
CBU-52 cluster bomb	6"/15CM	SALVO		2	6	One Shot

Crew: 1 - pilot
Weight: 23 tonnes
Length: 16.25m (53')
Wingspan: 17.53m (57'6")

Weapon: 30mm GAU-8/A cannon
Armour: Titanium bathtub
Speed: 681 Km/h (423 mph)
Engines: 2 × TF34-GE-100A turbofans

TEAM YANKEE
AH-1 COBRA ATTACK HELICOPTER PLATOON

AH-1 COBRA ATTACK HELICOPTER PLATOON	
4x AH-1 Cobra	**14 POINTS**
2x AH-1 Cobra	**7 POINTS**

The AH-1S Cobra is the latest version of the Vietnam-era Hueycobra and is easily distinguishable by its flatter, non-reflective canopy and the four Improved TOW missiles tubes mounted on each side.

This Cobra is a tank hunter, relying on its narrow frontal profile, the long reach of the Improved TOW missile, and skilful flying to remain undetected as it hunts its prey. The Cobra's chin-mounted M197 20mm Gatling gun makes short work of infantry and lightly-armoured vehicles, and any enemy helicopters it may come across.

• HELICOPTER AIRCRAFT UNIT • HUNTER-KILLER • THERMAL IMAGING•

COURAGE 4+	SKILL 4+
MORALE 4+	

IS HIT ON	AIRCRAFT SAVE
4+	**5+**

TACTICAL	TERRAIN DASH	CROSS COUNTRY DASH	ROAD DASH	CROSS
UNLIMITED				AUTO

WEAPON	RANGE	ROF HALTED	ROF MOVING	ANTI-TANK	FIRE-POWER	NOTES
Improved TOW missile	8"/20CM–48"/120CM	1	-	21	3+	Guided, HEAT
M197 20mm Vulcan Gatling gun	8"/20CM	6	3	6	5+	Anti-helicopter
M159 rocket launcher	16"/40CM	SALVO		4	6	One Shot

Crew: 2 - pilot, gunner
Weight: 5 tonnes
Length: 13.59m (45')
Rotor: 14.36m (48')

Weapons: M197 20mm Gatling gun
8x TOW missiles
Armour: Armoured windscreen
Speed: 227 Km/h (141 mph)

The 2nd Marine Division was formed during WWII and fought in the Pacific. In the 1950s and 60s it saw service in Lebanon, Cuba and the Dominican Republic. The division performed peacekeeping operations in Lebanon between 1982 and 1984 where 241 personnel were killed during the 1983 Beirut barracks bombing.

On 25 October 1983, the 22nd Marine Amphibious Unit (MAU), from the 2nd Marine Division, participated in the invasion of Grenada. The 22nd MAU conducted helicopter and surface landings over three days and occupied three-quarters of the island, even though the Marines made up less than one-fifth of the US force.

MARINES IN WORLD WAR III

In July 1985, the 2nd Marine Division was assigned to the US European Command as part of II Marine Amphibious Force. II Marine Amphibious Force (II MAF) is a Marine Air-Ground Task Force consisting of ground (2nd Marine Division), air (2nd Marine Aircraft Wing), and logistics forces capable of sustaining itself in combat without external assistance for up to 60 days.

With Norwegian and British forces holding the Soviets advancing in Norway, the II MAF, until then held for possible intervention in the north, was committed to support the NATO counterattack towards Bremen and Hamburg planned for 15 August. Taking advantage of their amphibious capabilities the Marines of II MAF were earmarked to land on the coast of Jutland, link up with West German and Danish forces, and push south into Schleswig-Holstein.

In the previous ten days Soviet and Polish forces had pushed up the Jutland Peninsula. Stiff defence by Danish and West German forces had slowed the advance and a defensive line had been formed across Jutland between Rejsby in the west, and the town of Haderslev in the east.

In the early hours of 15 August, the 2nd Marine Division began landing at Henne Strand, 30 km northwest of Varde, Denmark. With two of its three regiments ashore, the 2nd Marine Division quickly moved under the cover of darkness to Rejsby where they relieved the Danes holding that sector. With the 6th Marine Regiment still afloat, the 2nd Marine Regiment began the attack on the Soviet positions around Skærbæk at 0400 hours. While the 2nd Marine Regiment attacked, the 6th Marine Regiment began coming ashore in AAVP7 APCs further south along the coast near the village of Husum-Ballum, flanking the Soviet positions.

Soviet resistance was initially stiff, but after an hour of fighting they began to give ground. The M60 tanks from the 2nd Marine Tank Battalion provided support, making short work of Soviet BMPs and BTRs as they found them. The Marine tankers were soon pushing out ahead of the main advance, but were brought to a short stop when they encountered Soviet T-64 tanks at Døstrup. A number of M60 tanks were soon left burning in the fields approaching Døstrup.

As the morning progressed the division's Light Armoured Battalion, equipped with LAV 8-wheeled armoured vehicles, probed forward, calling on heavy fire support when needed. By mid-morning the Marines had advanced to the West German border and crossed at Aventoft, before advancing on Leck 22 km to the southeast.

The Marines encountered a Soviet blocking position north of Husum in the mid-afternoon. Air strikes and artillery pounded the position before the Marines engaged the enemy at Schwesing, a village to the west of Husum. A short, sharp battle through the streets pushed out the defenders.

Meanwhile, their West German and Danish NATO allies had taken Schleswig and were pushing on to Rendsburg. Directly to their front, the Soviets were withdrawing south-eastwards and taking positions behind the Nord-Ostsee Kanal. The Marines took Friedrichstadt, before bridging and crossing the Eider River. By early evening the division's leading element were closing in on Heide.

The 2nd Marine Division stormed across the Nord-Ostsee Kanal at Hohenhörn at about 2000 hours under the cover of artillery fire, establishing a bridgehead at the Hohenhörn ferry crossing on the eastern bank. The vehicle ferry itself had been scuttled during the Soviet advance, but the Marines' AAVP7 and LAV amphibious vehicles crossed. An Amphibious Bridging and Ferry unit attached from the West Germans began moving tanks and artillery across soon after.

The advance continued towards Itzehoe under the cover of darkness. News from NATO headquarters arrived that the offensive by the US 3rd Corps toward Bremen was going well, forcing Warsaw Pact units in the Netherlands to withdraw northwards to avoid being outflanked. However, at Itzehoe Soviet defences hardened. At about 0100 hours on 16 August, the Soviets directed an armoured counterattack on the 2nd Marine Division from Kellinghusen. Danish and West German forces were still working their way towards Neumünster, which Soviet forces free to attack the Marines' flank. A confused engagement developed in the darkness across the farmland east of Itzehoe. Close quarters fighting erupted at various spots across the front where Soviet motor riflemen had worked their way into the Marine's lines. After an hour of tough fighting the Soviets were forced to withdraw eastwards.

In the meantime, new orders arrived at division headquarters. The Soviet defence had stiffened around Bremen against the 3rd Corps's attack, so the Marines were ordered to conduct a diversionary attack from the north. A West German relieving force allowed the division to head for Glückstadt on the north bank of the Elbe. Utilising their amphibious vehicles and West German bridging equipment, they began crossing the river before sunrise.

The first light of 17 August saw the vanguard of the 2nd Marine Division assembled on the south bank of the Elbe, near Wischhafen. A Task Force of two battalions of the 8th Marine Regiment, two companies of the 2nd Marine Tank Battalion, and a company of LAVs from the 2nd Light Armored Vehicle Battalion led the advance. The LAV company began probing towards Osten, 15 km away on the banks of the Oste River. It wasn't long before they ran into enemy patrols.

A number of short clashes occurred as the LAVs ran into East German BRDM-2 scout cars along their advance towards Hemmoor. The LAVs easily outgunned the East German vehicles, who didn't stick around for a prolonged engagement.

On reaching Osten, it was discovered that the road bridge had been destroyed. The LAVs and the Marine riflemen in their AAVP7 amphibious APCs were able to cross in several places

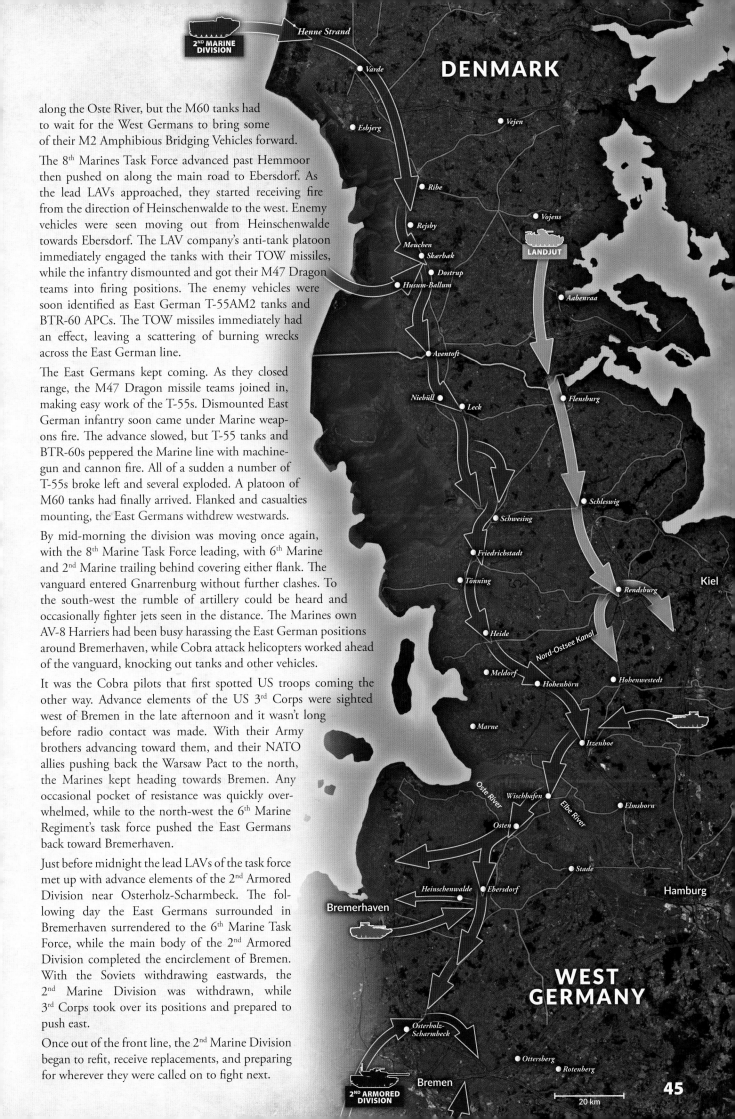

along the Oste River, but the M60 tanks had to wait for the West Germans to bring some of their M2 Amphibious Bridging Vehicles forward.

The 8th Marines Task Force advanced past Hemmoor then pushed on along the main road to Ebersdorf. As the lead LAVs approached, they started receiving fire from the direction of Heinschenwalde to the west. Enemy vehicles were seen moving out from Heinschenwalde towards Ebersdorf. The LAV company's anti-tank platoon immediately engaged the tanks with their TOW missiles, while the infantry dismounted and got their M47 Dragon teams into firing positions. The enemy vehicles were soon identified as East German T-55AM2 tanks and BTR-60 APCs. The TOW missiles immediately had an effect, leaving a scattering of burning wrecks across the East German line.

The East Germans kept coming. As they closed range, the M47 Dragon missile teams joined in, making easy work of the T-55s. Dismounted East German infantry soon came under Marine weapons fire. The advance slowed, but T-55 tanks and BTR-60s peppered the Marine line with machine-gun and cannon fire. All of a sudden a number of T-55s broke left and several exploded. A platoon of M60 tanks had finally arrived. Flanked and casualties mounting, the East Germans withdrew westwards.

By mid-morning the division was moving once again, with the 8th Marine Task Force leading, with 6th Marine and 2nd Marine trailing behind covering either flank. The vanguard entered Gnarrenburg without further clashes. To the south-west the rumble of artillery could be heard and occasionally fighter jets seen in the distance. The Marines own AV-8 Harriers had been busy harassing the East German positions around Bremerhaven, while Cobra attack helicopters worked ahead of the vanguard, knocking out tanks and other vehicles.

It was the Cobra pilots that first spotted US troops coming the other way. Advance elements of the US 3rd Corps were sighted west of Bremen in the late afternoon and it wasn't long before radio contact was made. With their Army brothers advancing toward them, and their NATO allies pushing back the Warsaw Pact to the north, the Marines kept heading towards Bremen. Any occasional pocket of resistance was quickly overwhelmed, while to the north-west the 6th Marine Regiment's task force pushed the East Germans back toward Bremerhaven.

Just before midnight the lead LAVs of the task force met up with advance elements of the 2nd Armored Division near Osterholz-Scharmbeck. The following day the East Germans surrounded in Bremerhaven surrendered to the 6th Marine Task Force, while the main body of the 2nd Armored Division completed the encirclement of Bremen. With the Soviets withdrawing eastwards, the 2nd Marine Division was withdrawn, while 3rd Corps took over its positions and prepared to push east.

Once out of the front line, the 2nd Marine Division began to refit, receive replacements, and preparing for wherever they were called on to fight next.

MARINE TANK COMPANY

Gunnery Sergeant Schrader felt the engine of his M60 strain as his tank began to grind up the slope. Since coming ashore on 15 August in Denmark, the 2nd Marine Tank Battalion had moved quickly until encountering Soviets near Husum-Ballum. The first enemy units had been BRDM-2 armoured cars that had scurried back into cover upon spotting the 50-ton Patton tanks. Their first kill had been a recon vehicle that reversed too far and lost the cover of the farm house it had been hiding behind. Now another more deadly threat had appeared, BMP-2 infantry fighting vehicles mounting AT-5 Spandrel ATGMs.

Schrader's platoon crested the ridge and began advancing towards Skærbæk, when the first missile launched towards them. Instantly, the tanks accelerated and changed direction trying to throw the enemy gunner off while spraying co-ax MG fire towards the launch point. The missile streaked behind another tank in the platoon, Sergeant Cunningham's tank, detonating in the distance. Schrader's gunner acquired the target, and the 105mm gun recoiled while the BMP burst into flames as the rear door blew off. More BMP's appeared and exchanged fire before withdrawing. Smouldering wrecks indicated those that had not withdrawn fast enough.

There was no warning missile contrail when Cunningham's tank detonated, the turret flying off to the side and a boiling column of thick oily smoke marking a pyre for the tank crew. Schrader urged his driver to get into cover as he scanned around for the new player — that had been a tank killer round. The platoon net came to life as Captain Ryan broadcast the news that Soviet T-64's had entered the battlefield.

Getting a kill shot on these Russian MBTs would need a flank shot. Schrader guided his driver down a narrow culvert until they were past the enemy, even as more M60's died in fiery conflagrations. The powerful engine surged again as they climbed the slope, leveling out with the rear aspect of three enemy tanks presented.

"Start on the left and work right. One round AP each. Engage!" In less than a minute the three enemy tanks were knocked out two in flames and one with hatches open and crew scattered around it.

"Semper Fi, Ivan".

A Marine division has one tank battalion to provide the armoured firepower to its three infantry regiments. A Marine tank battalion consists of four tank companies armed with M60A1 Patton tanks. Each of these companies can be reinforced with anti-tank and reconnaissance assets from the battalion headquarters.

The mission of the tank battalion and its subordinate tank companies is to close with and destroy the enemy by using their armoured firepower, shock effect, and manoeuvrability and to provide anti-armour fire support for the other formations of its Marine division.

As well as the Marine tank battalion operating as one manoeuvre force, the division commander may also organise task forces of tanks, mechanized infantry, and other division units based on the mission, enemy, terrain, weather, and troop availability. When organised in such a task force, and further supported by divisional artillery, strike aircraft and attack helicopters, the Marines can assemble a powerful combined arms force capable of operating independently or as part of a larger operation.

M60 PATTON TANK COMPANY

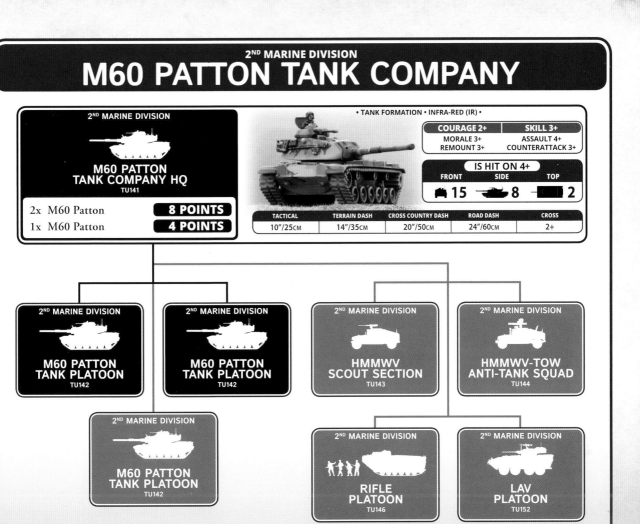

2ND MARINE DIVISION
M60 PATTON
TANK COMPANY HQ
TU141

• TANK FORMATION • INFRA-RED (IR) •

COURAGE 2+		SKILL 3+	
MORALE 3+		ASSAULT 4+	
REMOUNT 3+		COUNTERATTACK 3+	

IS HIT ON 4+		
FRONT	SIDE	TOP
15	8	2

2x M60 Patton	8 POINTS
1x M60 Patton	4 POINTS

TACTICAL	TERRAIN DASH	CROSS COUNTRY DASH	ROAD DASH	CROSS
10"/25CM	14"/35CM	20"/50CM	24"/60CM	2+

2ND MARINE DIVISION
M60 PATTON
TANK PLATOON
TU142

2ND MARINE DIVISION
M60 PATTON
TANK PLATOON
TU142

2ND MARINE DIVISION
HMMWV
SCOUT SECTION
TU143

2ND MARINE DIVISION
HMMWV-TOW
ANTI-TANK SQUAD
TU144

2ND MARINE DIVISION
M60 PATTON
TANK PLATOON
TU142

2ND MARINE DIVISION
RIFLE
PLATOON
TU146

2ND MARINE DIVISION
LAV
PLATOON
TU152

M60 PATTON TANK PLATOON

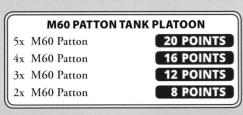

• TANK UNIT • INFRA-RED (IR) •

M60 PATTON TANK PLATOON	
5x M60 Patton	20 POINTS
4x M60 Patton	16 POINTS
3x M60 Patton	12 POINTS
2x M60 Patton	8 POINTS

COURAGE 3+		SKILL 4+	
MORALE 4+		ASSAULT 4+	
REMOUNT 3+		COUNTERATTACK 4+	

IS HIT ON 4+		
FRONT	SIDE	TOP
15	8	2

The US Marine Corps' main battle tank is the M60A1 Patton. Though it doesn't have all the upgrades of the Army's M60A3, it is still more than capable of dealing with any Warsaw Pact tanks it will encounter. The Marines' tank company is stronger than the Army equivalent with platoons of five tanks instead of four.

TACTICAL	TERRAIN DASH	CROSS COUNTRY DASH	ROAD DASH	CROSS
10"/25CM	14"/35CM	20"/50CM	24"/60CM	2+

WEAPON	RANGE	ROF HALTED	ROF MOVING	ANTI-TANK	FIRE-POWER	NOTES
M68 105mm gun	40"/100CM	2	2	20	2+	*Accurate, Stabiliser*
.50 cal MG	20"/50CM	3	2	4	5+	
7.62mm MG	16"/40CM	1	1	2	6	

HMMWV SCOUT SECTION

HMMWV SCOUT SECTION
1x HMMWV-M2
1x HMMWV-MK19
1x HMMWV-TOW | **2 POINTS**

A Marine tank battalion also has it own Scout Sections. These are mounted in the new HMMWV organised into sections of three vehicles, each armed with a different weapon. It has one HMMWV-M2 with a M2 .50 cal MG, one HMMWV-MK19 with a 40mm Mk19 grenade launcher, and one HMMWV-TOW with a Improved TOW anti-tank missile launcher.

• TANK UNIT • SCOUT • SPEARHEAD • THERMAL IMAGING •

COURAGE 3+	SKILL 4+
MORALE 4+	ASSAULT -
REMOUNT 3+	COUNTERATTACK -

IS HIT ON 4+

FRONT	SIDE	TOP
0	0	0

TACTICAL	TERRAIN DASH	CROSS COUNTRY DASH	ROAD DASH	CROSS
10"/25CM	12"/30CM	20"/50CM	40"/100CM	4+

WEAPON	RANGE	ROF HALTED	ROF MOVING	ANTI-TANK	FIRE-POWER	NOTES
HMMWV-M2 with .50 cal AA MG	20"/50CM	3	2	4	5+	
HMMWV-MK19 with 40mm grenade launcher	16"/40CM	5	4	4	6	
HMMWV-TOW with Improved TOW missile	8"/20CM–48"/120CM	1	-	21	3+	Guided, HEAT

HMMWV-TOW ANTI-TANK SQUAD

HMMWV-TOW ANTI-TANK SQUAD
2x HMMWV-TOW | **2 POINTS**

The Marines also use the improved TOW armed HMMWV in the anti-tank role in dedicated Anti-Tank Squads. These are mounted on the new HMMWV vehicle to provide mobility to keep pace with the tanks. The battalion then allocates anti-tank squads out to its tank companies as needed. Each anti-tank squad consists of two HMMWV-TOW vehicles.

• TANK UNIT • SCOUT • THERMAL IMAGING •

COURAGE 3+	SKILL 4+
MORALE 4+	ASSAULT 5+
REMOUNT 3+	COUNTERATTACK 6

IS HIT ON 4+

FRONT	SIDE	TOP
0	0	0

TACTICAL	TERRAIN DASH	CROSS COUNTRY DASH	ROAD DASH	CROSS
10"/25CM	12"/30CM	20"/50CM	40"/100CM	4+

WEAPON	RANGE	ROF HALTED	ROF MOVING	ANTI-TANK	FIRE-POWER	NOTES
Improved TOW missile	8"/20CM–48"/120CM	1	-	21	3+	Guided, HEAT

MARINE RIFLE COMPANY

"Janson! Beckdorf! Upstairs. Raulos, Chu - clear the other rooms. The rest cover the back - that's where they'll come from." Corporal Betzinger readied the grenade, then hurled it through the broken window. Like the rest of his squad, he pressed against the wall of the building, head bent and mouth open, waiting for the explosion. The Marines felt the blast wave hit them as smoke and shattered glass filled the air, Private Raulos kicked in the door and ducked in, spraying rounds. The rest of the unit piled in behind. A Soviet soldier staggered into view, his hold on his AK-74 drooping from the grenade concussion. A 3-round burst threw him back, collapsing to the floor.

Betzinger checked the bodies to make sure they wouldn't be getting back up and to look for any intel documents. Command were always harping about needing more intel. Two of the nearby buildings in Itzehoe were burning, providing the only light in the darkness. The Soviet counter-attack had hit the flank of the 6th Marines, and the fighting quickly turned into a confused mingling of friend and foe.

The thump of grenades, the chattering of automatic weapons fire, and wild streams of tracer fire suddenly erupted from the building two doors down.

"That must be Chavez. Watch for enemy trying to reinforce, knock 'em down before they can get in there." Heads bobbed in acknowledgement.

"Betz!" The yell came from upstairs.

"Movement across the street! Get ready!" Betzinger tapped each marine and indicated a direction to cover as he moved through the rooms. An enemy MG began firing from a 2nd floor window in the house opposite. Short bursts at each window and door, meant to keep his men suppressed, and heads down. He readied his last grenade and threw it out, the burst was accompanied by yells and cursing in Russian.

"Fire! Fire! Hose 'em!" he screamed, ramming his M-16 into his shoulder and firing controlled bursts into the charging enemy. Leaving half a dozen bodies behind, the enemy vanished back into the night.

A Marine division is based around a core of Marine infantry organised into three Marine infantry regiments. Each regiment usually consists of three Marine infantry battalions. These nine battalions each have three rifle companies, a weapons company and headquarters & service (H&S) company.

The H&S company provides intelligence, medical, service, and communications required by the battalion. The weapons company provides additional fire support elements for the rifle battalion like anti-tank and machine-guns.

The rifle companies are the fighting heart of a Marine forces. Each rifle company has three rifle platoons and a weapons platoon. The weapons platoon provides mortar, machine-gun and assault sections that are allocated out to the rifle platoons as needed for various combat missions.

Though the Marine rifle company has little transport of its own they can be provided with transport from the division's assault amphibian battalion AAVP7 assault amphibious vehicles or by the helicopters of the Marine aircraft group supporting their division. However, they are equally adapt at moving and fighting on foot.

The primary mission of the infantry battalion and its subordinate companies is to locate, close with, and destroy the enemy by fire and manoeuvre or to repel enemy attacks by fire and close combat.

RIFLE COMPANY

2ND MARINE DIVISION

RIFLE COMPANY HQ
TU145

1x M16 rifle team   **1 POINT**

The Formation Commander rides with one of the Rifle Platoons (TU146).

• INFANTRY FORMATION • HQ TRANSPORT • THERMAL IMAGING •

COURAGE 2+	SKILL 3+
MORALE 3+	ASSAULT 4+
RALLY 2+	COUNTERATTACK 3+

IS HIT ON	INFANTRY SAVE
4+	**3+**

TACTICAL	TERRAIN DASH	CROSS COUNTRY DASH	ROAD DASH	CROSS
8"/20CM	8"/20CM	12"/30CM	12"/30CM	AUTO

WEAPON	RANGE	ROF HALTED	ROF MOVING	ANTI-TANK	FIRE-POWER	NOTES
M16 rifle team	12"/30CM	2	1	1	5+	

2ND MARINE DIVISION

RIFLE PLATOON
TU146

2ND MARINE DIVISION

RIFLE PLATOON
TU146

2ND MARINE DIVISION

M60 PATTON TANK PLATOON
TU142

2ND MARINE DIVISION

LAV PLATOON
TU152

2ND MARINE DIVISION

RIFLE PLATOON
TU146

2ND MARINE DIVISION

HMMWV MACHINE-GUN PLATOON
TU150

2ND MARINE DIVISION

HMMWV-TOW ANTI-TANK SQUAD
TU144

2ND MARINE DIVISION
RIFLE PLATOON

COURAGE 3+	SKILL 4+
MORALE 4+	ASSAULT 4+
RALLY 3+	COUNTERATTACK 4+

IS HIT ON	INFANTRY SAVE
4+	3+

MARINE RIFLE PLATOON

9x M249 SAW team with
   M72 LAW anti-tank
2x AAVP7 (TU147)   **9 POINTS**

6x M249 SAW team with
   M72 LAW anti-tank
2x AAVP7 (TU147)   **6 POINTS**

OPTIONS

- Replace up to 2x M249 SAW team with M60 GPMG teams (TU148) at no cost.
- Add up to 2x M47 Dragon missile team (TU148) for +1 point each.
- Add 1x M224 60mm mortar team (TU148) for +1 point.
- Add up to 2x SMAW team (TU148) for +1 point each.
- Replace all AAVP7 with up to 4x UH-1 Huey (TU159) at no cost.

TACTICAL	TERRAIN DASH	CROSS COUNTRY DASH	ROAD DASH	CROSS
8"/20CM	8"/20CM	12"/30CM	12"/30CM	AUTO

WEAPON	RANGE	ROF HALTED	ROF MOVING	ANTI-TANK	FIRE-POWER	NOTES
M249 SAW team or M72 LAW anti-tank	12"/30CM	3	2	1	5+	
	12"/30CM	1	1	12	5+	HEAT, Slow Firing
M60 GPMG	16"/40CM	5	2	2	6	Assault 5

WEAPONS CARD

The Marine Rifle Platoon is a flexible unit with a wide variety of heavy weapons available. It has an additional card [TU148], with the data for its optional heavy support weapons.

WEAPON	RANGE	ROF HALTED	ROF MOVING	ANTI-TANK	FIRE-POWER	NOTES
M47 Dragon missile	8"/20CM–28"/70CM	1	-	18	3+	Assault 5, Guided, HEAT
SMAW team	16"/40CM	1	1	17	3+	Assault 5, HEAT, Slow Firing
M224 60mm mortar	32"/80CM	1	1	1	4+	Assault 5, Overhead Fire, Slow Firing

The main details for the Marine Rifle Platoon are on card TU146.

A Marine rifle platoon is organised into three rifle squads and a platoon headquarters. Each rifle squad has a squad leader and is divided into three four-man fire teams, one with a M249 Squad Automatic Weapon (SAW), a team leader with a M16 and a M203 grenade launcher, and two men with M16 assault rifles. The platoon headquarters consists of a platoon leader and three men all with M16 assault rifles.

When compared to the organisation of the Army's infantry, a Marine rifle platoon is a large and powerful unit with 43 men at full strength.

With the addition of elements from the company's weapons platoon and battalion's weapons company this could be further boasted with the addition of M60 general purpose machine-guns (GPMG), M47 Dragon anti-tank missile teams, M224 60mm mortars, and MK153 SMAW shoulder-launched multi-purpose assault weapons.

All this firepower combined with the *esprit de corps* and natural tenacity of the Marine rifleman will make a Marine rifle platoon hard to stop.

2ND MARINE DIVISION
AAVP7 TRANSPORT

The AAVP7 (Assault Amphibious Vehicle, Personnel Mark 7) is a fully tracked amphibious landing vehicle used by the assault amphibian battalions to land the infantry assault elements and equipment during amphibious operation. They can also conduct mechanized operations ashore.

The AAVP7 was upgraded to the AAVP7A1 to mount a turret armed with an M2 .50 cal heavy machine gun, and a 40mm Mk19 grenade launcher.

It has a crew of four and can carry up to 25 combat equipped Marines, allowing two vehicles to carry one Marine Rifle Platoon.

COURAGE 4+	SKILL 4+
MORALE 4+	ASSAULT 5+
REMOUNT 4+	COUNTERATTACK 5+

IS HIT ON 4+		
FRONT	SIDE	TOP
3	2	1

TACTICAL	TERRAIN DASH	CROSS COUNTRY DASH	ROAD DASH	CROSS
10"/25CM	18"/45CM	28"/70CM	32"/80CM	3+

WEAPON	RANGE	ROF HALTED	ROF MOVING	ANTI-TANK	FIRE-POWER	NOTES
40mm grenade launcher	16"/40CM	5	4	4	6	
.50 cal AA MG	20"/50CM	3	2	4	5+	

Crew: 4 - crew chief, driver, gunner, rear crewman
Weight: 26.4 tonnes
Length: 7.94m (26' 9.3")
Width: 3.27m (10' 8.72")
Height: 3.26 m (10' 10.5")
Armour: 45mm

Weapons: 40mm Mk19 grenade launcher
M2HB .50 cal MG
Engine: Cummins VTA-525 /903 cubic inches
300 kW (400 hp)
Speed: 32 km/h (20 mph)
Passengers: 25 combat equipped

UH-1 HUEY TRANSPORT HELICOPTER

DOOR GUNS: UH-1 Huey helicopters have door mounted M60 machine-guns to cover their passengers when they dismount and mount during air assault missions. Helicopters are vulnerable to enemy ground fire when coming into the landing zone, so unload and load quickly, and tend not to waste precious ammunition and time on other targets.

Unlike other Helicopters, UH-1 Huey's with Door Guns can Shoot while Landed. Door Guns can only Shoot in the turn that they Land.

• HELICOPTER AIRCRAFT ATTACHMENT • PASSENGERS 4 •

COURAGE 4+	SKILL 4+
MORALE 4+	

IS HIT ON	AIRCRAFT SAVE
4+	5+

TACTICAL	TERRAIN DASH	CROSS COUNTRY DASH	ROAD DASH	CROSS
UNLIMITED				AUTO

WEAPON	RANGE	ROF HALTED	MOVING	ANTI-TANK	FIRE-POWER	NOTES
Door M60 MGs	16"/40CM	4	4	2	6	Door Guns

The Marine light/attack helicopter squadrons provide the Marines with light utility helicopters, as well as Cobra attack helicopters, that can be used to transport Marine rifle platoons to and from the combat zone.

The UH-1N Hueys of the Marine Corps are fitted with M60 door machine-guns to give covering fire while loading and unloading passengers.

HMMWV MACHINE-GUN PLATOON

HMMWV MACHINE-GUN PLATOON

6x	HMMWV-M2	**4 POINTS**
3x	HMMWV-M2	**2 POINTS**

OPTIONS
• Replace any or all HMMWV-M2 with HMMWV-MK19 at no cost.

The machine-guns of the battalion weapons company are mounted on HMMWV weapons carriers. This platoon is equipped with both M2 .50cal heavy machine-guns and 40mm Mk19 automatic grenade launchers, so the commander and crew select which weapon to use depending on the mission.

• TANK UNIT •

COURAGE 3+	SKILL 4+
MORALE 4+	ASSAULT 6
REMOUNT 3+	COUNTERATTACK 6

IS HIT ON 4+		
FRONT	SIDE	TOP
0	0	0

TACTICAL	TERRAIN DASH	CROSS COUNTRY DASH	ROAD DASH	CROSS
10"/25CM	12"/30CM	20"/50CM	40"/100CM	4+

WEAPON	RANGE	ROF HALTED	MOVING	ANTI-TANK	FIRE-POWER	NOTES
HMMWV-M2 with .50 cal AA MG	20"/50CM	3	2	4	5+	
HMMWV-MK19 with 40mm grenade launcher	16"/40CM	5	4	4	6	

52

MARINE LAV COMPANY
(LIGHT ARMORED VEHICLE COMPANY)

The outlying buildings of Osten were welcoming cover for Sergeant Crosswell, as his LAV swerved to avoid yet another abandoned vehicle.

"Slow down Daniels! This isn't a DeLorean!" He swore viciously as they bumped over a kerb, rattling everyone inside. A block down the street, a squat, green 4-wheeled armoured car fired a burst of MG fire in their direction before scuttling out of sight.

"Contact! Enemy vehicle!" He passed the news on via the platoon network, then dropped into the turret. "Driver - advance to the corner. Gunner - standby."

The LAV edged up. More MG fire spattered off the front glacis. Brooks, the gunner, was already laying the M242 25mm Bushmaster chain-gun on to the fleeing target and firing a controlled burst. Rounds skipped along the tarmac before slamming into the BRDM-2, punching holes in the thin armour. The Soviet vehicle veered into a stationery Mercedes and came to a crashing halt. One crew member bailed out and huddled behind the wrecks. Another LAV, commanded by Corporal Killian, appeared further along and began to slowly advance. A sudden flash announced the impact of an AT missile, followed by an explosion of smoke, flame, and debris. A single trooper staggered out, beating at his smouldering uniform.

"Driver - go right! We need to find that shooter!" Daniels accelerated, smashing through a full height plate glass window, sending plastic furniture flying, before careening through another display window in a spray of sparkling shards. Another Soviet armoured car with a rack of missiles mounted on top was frantically turning around to escape. Brooks gave it no chance, tracking in front of the enemy and allowing them to drive into the stream of cannon shells. The enemy blew apart, chassis disintegrating, with wheels wobbling crazily away leaving a trail of burning rubber.

"Great Scott! It's gone back - to the future!" The hysterical laughter disguised the fear and relief they all felt at surviving another encounter with the enemy.

In the early 1980s, the US Marine Corps began looking for a light armoured vehicle to give their divisions greater mobility. They chose the Light Armored Vehicle (LAV) based on the Swiss MOWAG Piranha. In 1983, the 1st Light Armored Vehicle Battalion was created at Marine Corps Air and Ground Combat Center at Twentynine Palms, California to further test the vehicle capabilities and to establish a tactical doctrine. The first battalion equipped with the LAV-25 assigned to a division was the 2nd Light Armored Vehicle Battalion to the 2nd Marine Division. It began receiving its first LAVs in June 1984. The battalion's call sign was 'Wolfpack'.

The LAVs were assigned the reconnaissance role, taking on the same role as the cavalry battalions in the Army divisions. This involves conducting reconnaissance and security, and in given situations limited offensive or defensive operations that exploit the unit's mobility and firepower.

2ND MARINE DIVISION
LAV COMPANY

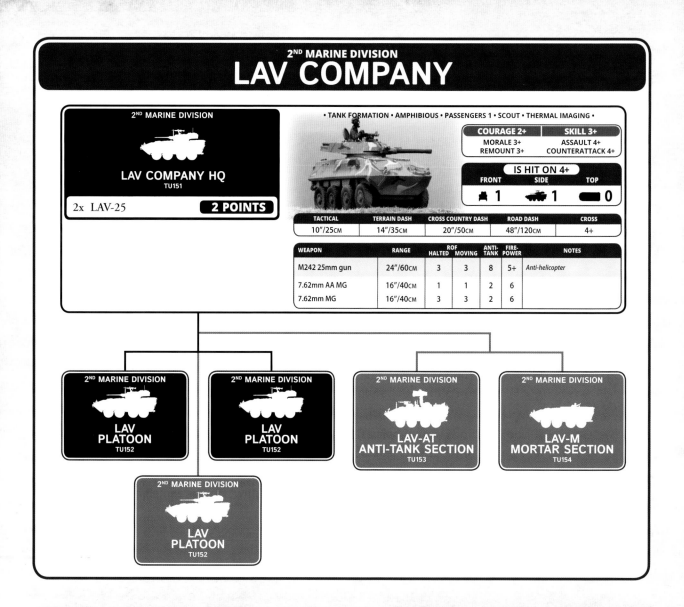

2ND MARINE DIVISION

LAV COMPANY HQ
TU151

2x LAV-25 — **2 POINTS**

• TANK FORMATION • AMPHIBIOUS • PASSENGERS 1 • SCOUT • THERMAL IMAGING •

COURAGE 2+	SKILL 3+
MORALE 3+	ASSAULT 4+
REMOUNT 3+	COUNTERATTACK 4+

IS HIT ON 4+

FRONT	SIDE	TOP
1	1	0

TACTICAL	TERRAIN DASH	CROSS COUNTRY DASH	ROAD DASH	CROSS
10"/25CM	14"/35CM	20"/50CM	48"/120CM	4+

WEAPON	RANGE	ROF HALTED	ROF MOVING	ANTI-TANK	FIRE-POWER	NOTES
M242 25mm gun	24"/60CM	3	3	8	5+	*Anti-helicopter*
7.62mm AA MG	16"/40CM	1	1	2	6	
7.62mm MG	16"/40CM	3	3	2	6	

2ND MARINE DIVISION
LAV PLATOON
TU152

2ND MARINE DIVISION
LAV PLATOON
TU152

2ND MARINE DIVISION
LAV-AT ANTI-TANK SECTION
TU153

2ND MARINE DIVISION
LAV-M MORTAR SECTION
TU154

2ND MARINE DIVISION
LAV PLATOON
TU152

2ND MARINE DIVISION
LAV PLATOON

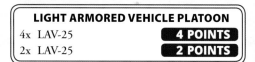

LIGHT ARMORED VEHICLE PLATOON	
4x LAV-25	**4 POINTS**
2x LAV-25	**2 POINTS**

• TANK UNIT • AMPHIBIOUS • SCOUT • SPEARHEAD • THERMAL IMAGING •

COURAGE 3+	SKILL 4+
MORALE 4+	ASSAULT 4+
REMOUNT 3+	COUNTERATTACK 5+

IS HIT ON 4+

FRONT	SIDE	TOP
1	1	0

TACTICAL	TERRAIN DASH	CROSS COUNTRY DASH	ROAD DASH	CROSS
10"/25CM	14"/35CM	20"/50CM	48"/120CM	4+

WEAPON	RANGE	ROF HALTED	ROF MOVING	ANTI-TANK	FIRE-POWER	NOTES
M242 25mm gun	24"/60CM	3	3	8	5+	*Anti-helicopter*
7.62mm AA MG	16"/40CM	1	1	2	6	
7.62mm MG	16"/40CM	3	3	2	6	

The Light Armored Vehicle, or LAV, is one of the newest vehicles in the Marine Corps' arsenal. Based on the Swiss MOWAG Piranha and built by General Motors in Canada, this vehicle offers the Marines a fast, highly mobile reconnaissance and light fire support vehicle.

Introduced in 1983, the Marine Corps have organised a number of light armored vehicle battalions equipped with the LAV and assigned to the Marine divisions. Each battalion has four light armored vehicle companies equipped with LAV-25, LAV-AT and LAV-M vehicles.

The standard LAV-25 found in the light armored vehicle platoons mounts a turret armed with an M242 25mm chain gun that can fire anti-tank and high-explosive rounds. A coaxial M240 machine-gun is mounted alongside the chain-gun, and a pintle-mounted M240 machine-gun is mounted on the turret roof.

LAV-AT ANTI-TANK SECTION

LAV-AT ANTI-TANK SECTION	
4x LAV-AT	**6 POINTS**
2x LAV-AT	**3 POINTS**

each light armored vehicle company has its own anti-tank vehicles in the form of the LAV-AT. The LAV-AT mounts the same Improved TOW Hammerhead launcher as found in the Army's M901 ITV anti-tank vehicle on the 8-wheeled LAV hull.

A LAV-AT anti-tank section consists of four LAV-AT vehicles.

• TANK UNIT • AMPHIBIOUS • HAMMERHEAD • SCOUT • THERMAL IMAGING •

COURAGE 3+	SKILL 4+
MORALE 4+	ASSAULT 5+
REMOUNT 3+	COUNTERATTACK 5+

IS HIT ON 4+		
FRONT	SIDE	TOP
1	1	0

TACTICAL	TERRAIN DASH	CROSS COUNTRY DASH	ROAD DASH	CROSS
10"/25CM	14"/35CM	20"/50CM	48"/120CM	4+

WEAPON	RANGE	ROF HALTED	ROF MOVING	ANTI-TANK	FIRE-POWER	NOTES
Improved TOW missile	8"/20CM - 48"/120CM	1	-	21	3+	*Guided, HEAT*
7.62mm AA MG	16"/40CM	3	3	2	6	

LAV-M MORTAR SECTION

LAV-M MORTAR SECTION	
2x LAV-M	**2 POINTS**

For smoke and immediate fire support the light armored vehicle company can call on its pair of LAV-Ms. The LAV-M is an un-turreted LAV with an 81mm mortar mounted in its rear passenger compartment. A large hatched opening in the top rear of the vehicle allows the mortar to fire from its protected position inside the LAV-M.

• TANK UNIT • AMPHIBIOUS • THERMAL IMAGING •

COURAGE 3+	SKILL 4+
MORALE 4+	ASSAULT 5+
REMOUNT 3+	COUNTERATTACK 5+

IS HIT ON 4+		
FRONT	SIDE	TOP
1	1	0

TACTICAL	TERRAIN DASH	CROSS COUNTRY DASH	ROAD DASH	CROSS
10"/25CM	14"/35CM	20"/50CM	48"/120CM	4+

WEAPON	RANGE	ROF HALTED	ROF MOVING	ANTI-TANK	FIRE-POWER	NOTES
81mm Mortar	56"/140CM	ARTILLERY		1	4+	*Smoke Bombardment*
7.62mm AA MG	16"/40CM	3	3	2	6	

MARINE SUPPORT

2ND MARINE DIVISION
M109 ARTILLERY BATTERY

M109 ARTILLERY BATTERY	
6x M109	**14 POINTS**
3x M109	**7 POINTS**

OPTIONS
- Arm all M109 with Bomblets for +1 point.
- Arm all M109 with Minelets for +1 point.
- Arm all M109 with Laser-Guided Projectiles for +1 point each.

In 1978 each Marine divisions received a battalion of M109 155mm self-propelled howitzers to supplement their more static 155mm towed howitzers.

• TANK UNIT • BOMBLETS • LASER-GUIDED PROJECTILES • MINELETS •

COURAGE 3+	SKILL 4+
MORALE 4+	ASSAULT 5+
REMOUNT 3+	COUNTERATTACK 5+

IS HIT ON 4+

FRONT	SIDE	TOP
2	2	1

TACTICAL	TERRAIN DASH	CROSS COUNTRY DASH	ROAD DASH	CROSS
10"/25CM	16"/40CM	24"/60CM	28"/70CM	3+

WEAPON	RANGE	ROF HALTED	ROF MOVING	ANTI-TANK	FIRE-POWER	NOTES
M185 155mm howitzer	96"/240CM	ARTILLERY		4	2+	*Smoke Bombardment*
or Direct fire	36"/90CM	1	1	15	1+	*Brutal, Slow Firing, Smoke*
.50 cal AA MG	20"/50CM	3	2	4	5+	

2ND MARINE DIVISION
HMMWV OBSERVATION POST

HMMWV OBSERVATION POST	
1x HMMWV OP	**1 POINT**

You must field:
- *a 2nd Marine Division M109 Marine Artillery Battery* (TU156)

before you may field a 2nd Marine Division HMMWV OP.

The Marine artillery observers have traded their jeeps in for the HMMWV. This new vehicle allows them to seek good positions in cover from which to call down the artillery.

• INDEPENDENT TANK UNIT • OBSERVER • SCOUT • THERMAL IMAGING •

COURAGE 3+	SKILL 4+
MORALE 4+	ASSAULT 5+
REMOUNT 3+	COUNTERATTACK 5+

IS HIT ON 4+

FRONT	SIDE	TOP
0	0	0

TACTICAL	TERRAIN DASH	CROSS COUNTRY DASH	ROAD DASH	CROSS
10"/25CM	12"/30CM	20"/50CM	40"/100CM	4+

WEAPON	RANGE	ROF HALTED	ROF MOVING	ANTI-TANK	FIRE-POWER	NOTES
.50 cal AA MG	20"/50CM	3	2	4	5+	

2ND MARINE DIVISION
AV-8 HARRIER ATTACK FLIGHT

AV-8 HARRIER ATTACK FLIGHT	
4x AV-8 Harrier	**6 POINTS**
2x AV-8 Harrier	**3 POINTS**

The US Marine Corps adopted the British Hawker-Siddley Harrier, the famed 'Jump Jet', in 1971. Designated AV-8, the Harrier is a high performance jet aircraft that is uniquely capable of vertical and short take off and landing (VSTOL). It does this by swivelling its exhaust nozzles down to allow it to take off vertically.

The Marines can operate their Harriers from aircraft carriers as well as light assault ships. Once inland the Harriers operate from forward bases, containing one to four aircraft, located 20 miles (32 km) from the front, while a more established airbase would be located around

• STRIKE AIRCRAFT UNIT • JUMP JET •

COURAGE 3+	SKILL 4+
MORALE 4+	

IS HIT ON	AIRCRAFT SAVE
4+	**5+**

TACTICAL	TERRAIN DASH	CROSS COUNTRY DASH	ROAD DASH	CROSS
UNLIMITED				AUTO

WEAPON	RANGE	ROF HALTED	ROF MOVING	ANTI-TANK	FIRE-POWER	NOTES
30mm Aden gun	8"/20CM	-	3	7	5+	*Anti-helicopter*
CBU-100 cluster bomb	6"/15CM	SALVO		7	5+	

50 miles (80 km) from the front. The forward bases allow for a far greater sortie rate and reduced fuel consumption.

Armed with a electrically-powered 30mm Aden 5-chamber revolver cannon and CBU-100 cluster bombs, the Harrier can deal with both air and ground targets.

SPECIAL RULES

JUMP JET

The AV-8 Harrier jump jet can get airborne with a full armament load after a short take-off run. This allows it to operate from hidden locations near the front, like supermarket car parks, enabling them to quickly rearm and return to the front after a sortie.

> Jump Jet Strike Aircraft arrive each turn on a roll of 3+, rather than the usual 4+.

DOOR GUNS

UH-1 Huey helicopters have door mounted M60 machine-guns to cover their passengers when they dismount and mount during air assault missions. Helicopters are vulnerable to enemy ground fire when coming into the landing zone, so unload and load quickly, and tend not to waste precious ammunition and time on other targets.

> Unlike other Helicopters, UH-1 Hueys with Door Guns can Shoot while Landed. Door Guns can only Shoot in the turn that they Land.

RADAR

Anti-aircraft radars make tracking fast-moving aircraft much easier, especially at long range.

> When Shooting at Aircraft, vehicles equipped with Radar do not suffer the usual +1 penalty To Hit for range over 16"/40cm and extend their range to:
>
> * 36"/90cm for a **M247 Sergeant York**,
> * 32"/80cm for a **M163 VADS**.

SCENARIOS

As well as playing the missions in the Team Yankee rulebook, or downloaded from the website *www.Team-Yankee.com*, you can also play scenarios inspired by your imagination, your favourite WWIII fiction, or even historical battles put into a WWIII context.

The following three scenarios are based on the actions of 1st and 2nd Brigades of the 1st Armored Division.

You can play them as a one-off action or in order, using the Consequences and Campaign sections to carry forward the results from one game to another. You can swap sides and play through the campaign to compare your forces and your approaches.

There is also no reason why you can't play all the scenarios with different forces. You can even try different terrain arrangements, as terrain can often make all the difference to how a game plays.

Most importantly of all, have fun and feel free to modify the scenarios anyway you see fit.

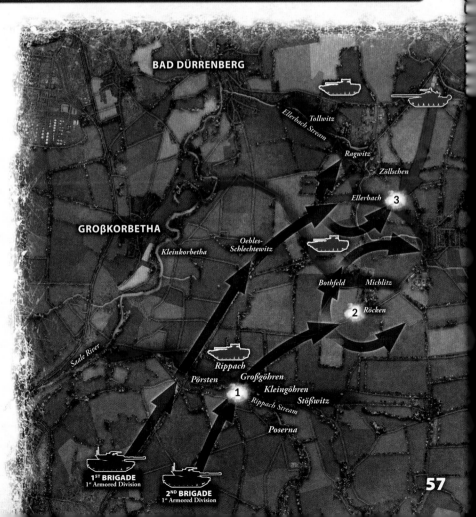

1

RIPPACH STREAM

Captain William 'Buck' Taylor peered at his thermal imaging display as he searched the tree line ahead for the enemy. Out in front, he could see the small, light coloured blobs of the mech infantry advancing dismounted towards the village that straddled the tree-lined stream ahead. The sudden appearance of a bright area on the mono-tone green screen caught his attention.

"Target, tank, 3 o'clock, 700 metres," he called to his gunner.

"Up," his loader signalled to the gunner that a round was in the breech.

"On the way," the gunner called as the tank wobbled slightly with the gun firing.

A bright flash in his display announced the accuracy of the shot. Buck then began scanning the distance for their next target.

Captain Buck Taylor's Combat Team Alpha, along with the rest of the 2nd Brigade, 1st Armored Division, advanced through the darkness towards the Rippach Stream and the villages of Rippach and Großgöhren. Their goal is to push through and head towards Lützen, leaving the clearing of the villages to the mech infantry battalions behind them.

Your IPM1 Armored Combat Team is to destroy any enemy armour and push through the line of villages to fields and roads leading to Lützen.

SPECIAL RULES

• Ambush (see page 100 of Team Yankee)

• Night Fighting (see page 66 of Team Yankee)

The entire game is played with the Night Fighting rules.

SETTING UP

Lay out the terrain on a 6' x 4' (180cm s 120cm) table as shown on the map on the following page.

Place an Objective on each of the spots marked ⊗.

DEPLOYMENT

The Soviet SU-25 Frogfoot Aviation Company starts the game Loitering Off Table (see page 30 of Team Yankee), but cannot come on until Soviet Turn 2. The Storm Anti-tank Platoon is held in Ambush. The remainder of the Soviet force is deployed on table in the Soviet Deployment area marked on the table in front of the Objectives. Soviet infantry teams may start the game in Foxholes (see pages 35, 48, and 54 of Team Yankee).

The US force is then deployed on the table in the US deployment area.

STARTING THE GAME

The US Player is the Attacker and has the first turn.

WINNING THE GAME

The US Player wins the game if they start any turn Holding any of the Objectives.

The Soviet players wins at the start of any turn from Turn 6 with no US teams within 8"/20cm of either Objective.

CONSEQUENCES

If the US player wins, they will have broken through the line of villages on the Rippach Stream and then pushed on towards Lützen. If the Soviet player wins they have delayed the US advance, allowing for further reinforcements to arrive.

WHAT HAPPENED

Buck Taylor's Team Alpha, along with the rest of the brigade, was able to punch a hole through the Soviet defences at Rippach and Großgöhren to then head towards Lützen. The 1st Brigade, 1st Infantry Division then mopped up the remaining Soviet defenders along the Rippach Stream.

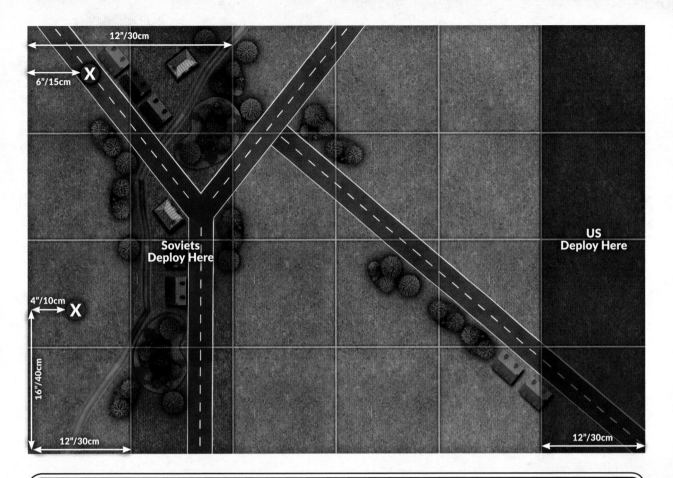

FORCES

M1 ABRAMS ARMORED COMBAT TEAM

M1 Abrams Armored Combat Team HQ
    2x IPM1 Abrams

M1 Abrams Tank Platoon
    4x IPM1 Abrams

M1 Abrams Tank Platoon
    4x IPM1 Abrams

M113 Mech Platoon
    4x M249 SAW team with M72 LAW anti-tank
    3x M47 Dragon missile team
    4x M113

M247 Sergeant York AA Platoon (Support Unit)
    2x M247 Sergeant York

ALTERNATIVE FORCE: 98 POINTS

BMP MOTOR RIFLE BATTALION

BMP Motor Rifle Battalion HQ
    1x AK-74 team
    1x BMP-2

BMP-2 Motor Rifle Company
    7x AK-74 team with RPG-18 anti-tank
    6x RPG-7 Anti-tank team
    2x PKM LMG team
    9x BMP-2

BMP-2 Motor Rifle Company
    7x AK-74 team with RPG-18 anti-tank
    6x RPG-7 Anti-tank team
    2x PKM LMG team
    9x BMP-2

T-64 Tank Company
    6x T-64 with AT-8 Songster missiles

IN AMBUSH

Storm Anti-tank Platoon (Support Unit)
    3x Storm

LOITERING OFF TABLE UNTIL TURN 2

SU-25 Frogfoot Aviation Company (Support Unit)
    2x SU-25 Frogfoot

ALTERNATIVE FORCE: 81 POINTS

2

RÖCKEN

A resounding crash echoed though the turret. Lieutenant Andersen's ears were left ringing as he concentrated to hear what his gunner was saying through the tank's intercom.

"What? Repeat," he asked as the ringing began to subside.

"...o damage. It hit the turret front, the armour held, and everything seems good," his gunner repeated.

This new IPM1 tank was proving to be one tough beast.

"We better not leave that unanswered, let's find that bastard and return the favour!"

They soon found their tormentor concealed among some farm buildings, along with a few of his friends. The bright glow of their warm engines giving them away through the darkness.

Having broken through the Soviet line on the Rippach Stream, Captain Buck Taylor's Combat Team Alpha is leading the way of 2nd Brigade, 1st Armored Division, towards Lützen, when it comes under fire approaching the villages of Bothfeld, Michlitz and Röcken. The 2nd of the 37th Battalion returns fire, while the rest of the brigade swings left and right to encircle the Soviet positions. The mech infantry of the 2nd of the 6th Battalion then assaults the villages.

Your IPM1 Armored Combat Team is to eliminate Soviet resistance in Röcken, before supporting the mech infantry while they clear the village of resistance.

SPECIAL RULES

• Ambush (see page 100 of Team Yankee)

• Delayed Reserves (see page 100 of Team Yankee)

• Night Fighting (See page 66 of Team Yankee)

The entire game is played with the Night Fighting rules.

SETTING UP

Lay out the terrain on a 6' x 4' (180cm s 120cm) table as shown on the map on the following page.

Place an Objective on each of the spots marked .

DEPLOYMENT

The Storm Anti-tank Platoon is held in Ambush. The smaller BMP-2 Motor Rifle Company and T-64 Tank Company are held in Delayed Reserve and arrive along the Soviet player's table edge. The remainder of the Soviet force is deployed on table in the Soviet Deployment area marked on the table.

The US force is then deployed on the table in the US deployment area.

STARTING THE GAME

The US Player is the Attacker and has the first turn.

WINNING THE GAME

The US Player wins the game if they start any turn Holding any of the Objectives.

The Soviet players wins at the start of any turn from Turn 6 with no US teams within 8"/20cm of either Objective.

CAMPAIGN

If the Soviet player won *Rippach Stream*, the US player must play *Röcken* without the M106 Heavy Mortar Platoon.

If the US player won *Rippach Stream*, the Soviet player does not have time to fully prepare their defence. The Storm Anti-tank Platoon is not placed in Ambush. It is instead deployed on the table with the other Soviet units.

CONSEQUENCES

If the US player wins, they have broken through another Soviet position in front of Lützen, the town now lies in sight beyond the village of Röcken. If the Soviet player wins they have bought further time to better prepare their defences around Lützen.

WHAT HAPPENED

The assault on the villages of Bothfeld, Michlitz and Röcken became bogged down in fighting for over an hour as the US mech infantry had to root out every last pocket of stubborn resistance.

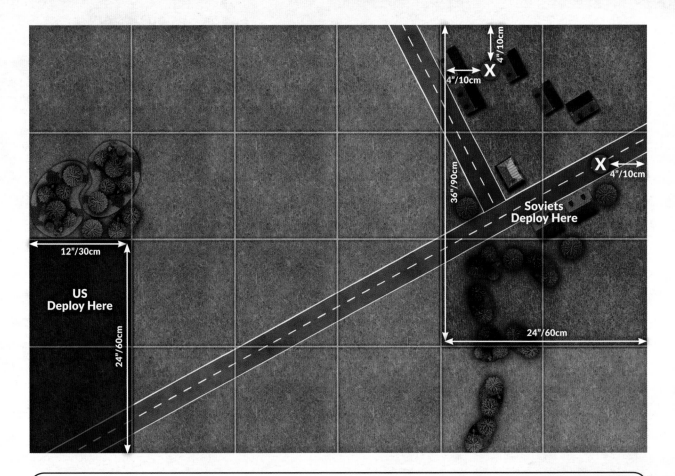

FORCES

BATTALION COMBAT TEAM

M1 Abrams Armored Combat Team HQ
  2x IPM1 Abrams

M1 Abrams Tank Platoon
  4x IPM1 Abrams

M1 Abrams Tank Platoon
  3x IPM1 Abrams

M106 Heavy Mortar Platoon
  3x M106

M113 Mech Combat Team HQ
  1x M16 rifle team
  1x M113

M113 Mech Platoon
  4x M249 SAW team with M72 LAW anti-tank
  3x M47 Dragon missile team
  4x M113

M113 Mech Platoon
  4x M249 SAW team with M72 LAW anti-tank
  3x M47 Dragon missile team
  4x M113

M901 ITV Anti-tank Platoon
  2x M901 ITV

ALTERNATIVE FORCE: 100 POINTS

MOTOR RIFLE REGIMENT

BMP Motor Rifle Battalion HQ
  1x AK-74 team
  1x BMP-2

BMP-2 Motor Rifle Company
  10x AK-74 team with RPG-18 anti-tank
  9x RPG-7 Anti-tank team
  2x PKM LMG team
  12x BMP-2

Spandrel Anti-tank Platoon
  3x Spandrel

T-64 Tank Battalion HQ
  1x T-64

T-64 Tank Company
  5x T-64 with AT-8 Songster missiles

IN AMBUSH

Storm Anti-tank Platoon (Support Unit)
  3x Storm

DELAYED RESERVES

BMP-2 Motor Rifle Company
  7x AK-74 team with RPG-18 anti-tank
  6x RPG-7 Anti-tank team
  2x PKM LMG team
  9x BMP-2

T-64 Tank Company
  4x T-64

ALTERNATIVE FORCE: 101 POINTS

3

ELLERBACH STREAM

The engine of the M60 tank roared as Sergeant Bain's driver put the power on and pushed across the stream. The big tank pushed up the far bank and through the bushes and small trees that lined the waterway. As the tank nosed down beyond the bank, Bain checked his thermal imaging display and was shocked to see a group of five or six Soviet tanks coming towards them from about a klick away.

"Targets, six T-64 tanks, ahead, engage," came the Lieutenant's voice across the platoon net.

"Pointing the out the obvious," muttered Bain to himself about his young platoon leader, "though, full points for recognition." Across the tank intercom he ordered, "Leroy, engage targets."

"Sabot on the way," Bain's gunner, Private Leroy Simmons, sent an anti-tank round to the first T-64, which exploded in a satisfying plume of fire, illuminating the rest of the Soviet unit.

While the battle for the villages of Bothfeld, Michlitz, and Röcken raged to the south-east, the tanks and mech infantry of the 1st Brigade, 1st Armored Division pushed along Autobahn 9 towards the string of villages that sat along the Ellerbach Stream. Pushing around the flank of the villages while the mech infantry engaged, are the M60 tanks of the 1st of the 37th Armor Battalion. They soon encounter a Soviet armoured counterattack coming the other way.

Your M60 Armored Combat Team is to destroy the Soviet counterattack and secure the 1st Brigade's flank.

SPECIAL RULES
• Night Fighting (See page 66 of Team Yankee)

The entire game is played with the Night Fighting rules.

SETTING UP
Lay out the terrain on a 6' x 4' (180cm x 120cm) table as shown on the map on the following page.

Place one Soviet Objective in the US Deployment and one US Objective in the Soviet Deployment on the spots marked **X**.

DEPLOYMENT
Starting with the US player, alternate deploying Units one at a time.

STARTING THE GAME
The US Player is the Attacker and has the first turn.

WINNING THE GAME
The US Player wins the game if they start any turn Holding the Objective in the Soviet deployment area.

The Soviet player wins the game if they start any turn Holding the Objective in the US deployment area.

CAMPAIGN
If the Soviet player won *Röcken*, the Soviet player adds a T-64 Tank Company of three T-64 tanks held in Immediate Reserves (see page 101 of Team Yankee) that arrives from the Soviet table edge.

If the US player won *Röcken*, the US player adds a second unit of two 901 ITVs to their force.

CONSEQUENCES
If the US player wins, they have stopped the Soviets' getting around the brigade's flank, allowing the mech infantry's attack to continue unhindered. If the Soviet player wins they have flanked the main attack and force the 1st Brigade to withdraw and regroup.

WHAT HAPPENED
The battle forces both tank forces to withdraw. However, it halted the Soviet armoured counterattack and the 1st or the 6th Mech Battalion was able to take the positions on the Ellerbach Stream and opened the way for the 1st Brigade, 1st Armored to push up Autobahn 9 towards Leipzig.

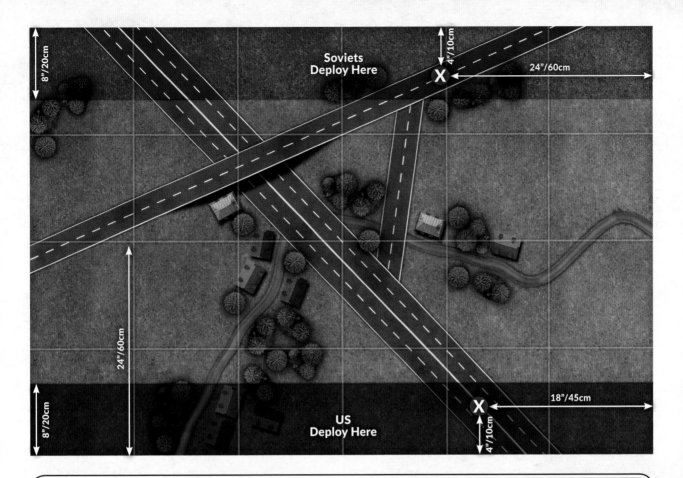

8"/20cm

4"/10cm

**Soviets
Deploy Here**

X

24"/60cm

24"/60cm

8"/20cm

18"/45cm

**US
Deploy Here**

X

4"/10cm

FORCES

M60 PATTON ARMORED COMBAT TEAM

M60 Patton Armored Combat Team HQ
    2x M60 Patton

M60 Patton Tank Platoon
    4x M60 Patton

M60 Patton Tank Platoon
    4x M60 Patton

M60 Patton Tank Platoon
    4x M60 Patton

M106 Heavy Mortar Platoon
    3x M106

M113 Mech Platoon
    4x M249 SAW team with M72 LAW anti-tank
    3x M47 Dragon missile team
    4x M113

M901 ITV Anti-tank Platoon
    2x M901 ITV

M113 Scout Section
    1x M113 Scout
    1x M901 ITV

AH-1 Cobra Attack Helicopter Platoon (Support Unit)
    2x AH-1 Cobra

ALTERNATIVE FORCE: 77 POINTS

T-64 TANK BATTALION

T-64 Tank Battalion HQ
    1x T-64

T-64 Tank Company
    5x T-64 with AT-8 Songster missiles

T-64 Tank Company
    5x T-64

T-64 Tank Company
    5x T-64

ZSU-23-4 Shilka AA Platoon
    2x ZSU-23-4 Shilka

BRDM-2 Recon Platoon
    2x BRDM-2

ALTERNATIVE FORCE: 86 POINTS

PAINTING US FORCES

US ARMOUR

M60
MERDC WINTER
VERDANT

M113 TRACK
MASSTER CAMOUFLAGE

The US Army experimented with a lot of different camouflage schemes during the 1970s and 80s. Visit out website, *www.Team-Yankee.com,* for more information on alternate camouflage schemes and colours.

US AIRCRAFT

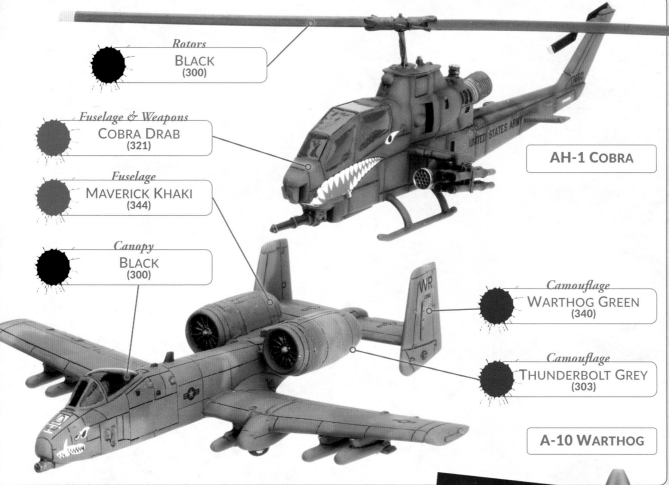

Rotors
BLACK
(300)

Fuselage & Weapons
COBRA DRAB
(321)

Fuselage
MAVERICK KHAKI
(344)

Canopy
BLACK
(300)

AH-1 COBRA

Camouflage
WARTHOG GREEN
(340)

Camouflage
THUNDERBOLT GREY
(303)

A-10 WARTHOG

This painting guide uses the *Colours Of War* painting system. *Colours of War,* the book, is a detailed and comprehensive guide to painting miniatures that shows you, step-by-step, everything you need to know to field beautifully painted miniatures in your *Team Yankee* games. While *Colours of War* focuses on the Second World War miniatures of *Flames Of War*, the techniques work just the same for *Team Yankee*.

Visit the *Team Yankee* website: www.Team-Yankee.com for more information.

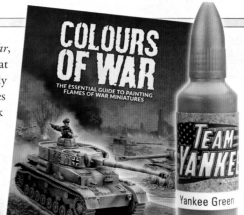

MERDC CAMOUFLAGE

COLOUR PALETTE

YANKEE GREEN
(350)

ORDNANCE SHADE
(492)

BATTLEFIELD BROWN
(324)

DRY DUST
(364)

BLACK
(300)

In the late 1970s, the US Army adopted the MERDC camouflage system (named for the Mobility Equipment Research and Development Center that developed it).

This sophisticated camouflage scheme could be varied for different environments.

The US forces in NATO normally used the Winter Verdant scheme shown on this page.

As MERDC was being phased out in favour of a new NATO standard camouflage scheme, new equipment was sometimes left in uncamouflaged green. So, if you don't want to tackle MERDC just yet, you can skip the fancy camouflage stages.

BATTLEFIELD BROWN
Large Brush

BASECOAT the tracks with Battfield Brown. Some people find it faster and easier to paint the tracke separately before gluing them onto the tank.

ORDNANCE SHADE
Large Brush

WASH the tracks with Ordnance Shade. Try to achieve an even coverage over the tracks, letting the wash pool in the recesses without building up too much on flat surfaces.

YANKEE GREEN
Large Brush

BASECOAT your tank with Yankee Green. Two thin coats are preferable to one thick coat. Alternatively, you can use a Yankee Green spray can for your undercoat.

BATTLEFIELD BROWN
Medium Brush

OUTLINE the camouflage pattern with Battlefield Brown, then fill in the outlines. It's a good idea to look at historical photographs for guidance.

DRY DUST
BLACK
Fine Brush

EDGE the Battlefield Brown camouflage with short branches of Dry Dust. These lines surround about a third of the edge of the camouflage colour. Then edge the camouflage patterns with 'gull wings' of Black. These patterns also surround about a third of the edge of the brown patches.

BLACK
Fine Brush

PAINT the track-pads and mud-guards Black. To add extra definition you can highlight the black with Worn Rubber.

DRY DUST
Drybrush

DRYBRUSH the tank with Dry Dust concentrating on edges, raised details, and upper surfaces to add highlight.

ORDNANCE SHADE
Fine Brush

WASH the details with Ordnance Shade to add definition to the camouflage pattern.

BASING US ARMY AND MARINE INFANTRY

All *Team Yankee* infantry are supplied with appropriate bases. Assemble your infantry teams by gluing the figures into the holes on a base of the right size. Super glue works well for this.

There are usually several figures with each type of weapon, so you can create variety in your squads. It doesn't matter which figure you put in each team, as long as the mix of weapons is right. Visit the product spotlight on the *Team Yankee* website: www.Team-Yankee.com for a more detailed guide.

Colours Of War has a complete basing guide for more information and lots of clever ideas.

Formation Commander M16 rifle team
Base the Commander on a small base with a radio operator and rifleman.

SMAW

M224 60mm mortar

M249 SAW team with M72 LAW anti-tank

Base an M249 SAW team on a medium base. Teams combine a machine-gunner armed with an M249 SAW squad automatic weapon, riflemen armed with M16 rifles and M72 LAW anti-tank weapons, and a grenadier armed with an M16 rifle and under-slung M203 grenade launcher.

Replace the M249 SAW and grenadier with an officer and radio operator for the Unit Leader.

M60 GPMG

Base M60 GPMG teams on a medium base. Teams combine an M60 gunner with two rifle armed assistants.

M47 Dragon

Base M47 Dragon missile teams, 60mm Mortar teams and SMAW teams on a small base. Each base has one gunner and one loader miniature

PAINTING US ARMY AND MARINE INFANTRY

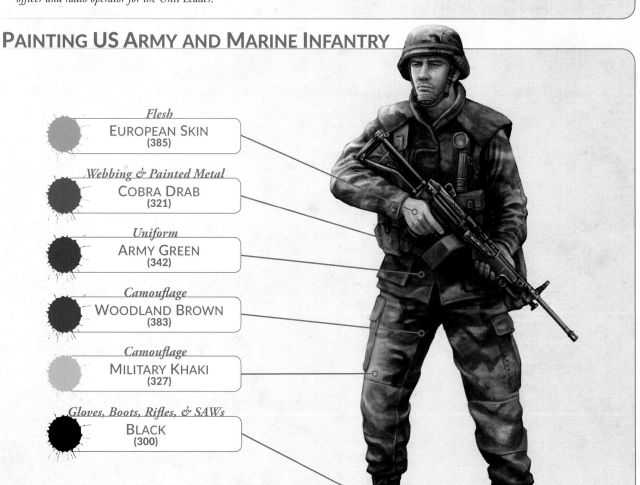

Flesh
EUROPEAN SKIN
(385)

Webbing & Painted Metal
COBRA DRAB
(321)

Uniform
ARMY GREEN
(342)

Camouflage
WOODLAND BROWN
(383)

Camouflage
MILITARY KHAKI
(327)

Gloves, Boots, Rifles, & SAWs
BLACK
(300)

Camouflage Uniforms

Colour Palette

Army Green
(342)

Ordnance Shade
(492)

Woodland Brown
(483)

Military Khaki
(327)

Black
(300)

US soldiers wore camou-flaged BDU (Battle Dress Uniform) in the standard woodland camouflage pattern.

ARMY GREEN — *Large Brush*

BASECOAT *the uniform with Army Green, using two thin coats if necessary to achieve an even coverage.*

ORDNANCE SHADE — *Large Brush*

WASH *the figure liberally with Ordnance Shade to add depth to the uniform.*

WOODLAND BROWN — *Fine Brush*

CAMOUFLAGE *with small patches of Woodland Brown covering about one-third of the uniform.*

MILITARY KHAKI — *Fine Brush*

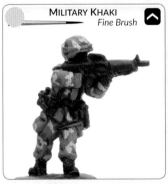

CAMOUFLAGE *with small patches of Military Khaki covering about half of the remaining Army Green.*

BLACK — *Fine Brush*

CAMOUFLAGE *with fine lines of Black across the Woodland Brown and Military Khaki.*

ORDNANCE SHADE — *Fine Brush*

ACTUAL SIZE

PINWASH *some of the deep recesses with Ordnance Shade to add more depth.*

Webbing Equipment

Colour Palette

Cobra Green
(321)

Ordnance Shade
(492)

COBRA GREEN — *Medium Brush*

BASECOAT *the webbing with Cobra Green.*

ORDNANCE SHADE — *Fine Brush*

WASH *the details carefully with Ordnance Shade.*

COBRA GREEN — *Fine Brush*

ACTUAL SIZE

TIDY UP *with another layer of Cobra Green.*

Skin

Colour Palette

European Skin
(385)

Skin Shade
(491)

Use Leather Brown for African-American skin.

EUROPEAN SKIN — *Medium Brush*

BASECOAT *the face and hands with European Skin, in two thin coats.*

SKIN SHADE — *Medium Brush*

WASH *liberally with Skin Shade to create shading and definition.*

EUROPEAN SKIN — *Fine Brush*

ACTUAL SIZE

HIGHLIGHT *raised details such as fingers and nose with European Skin.*

TUSABX2
BANNON'S BOYS

Bannon's Boys contains all the American models you need to begin building an M1 or IPM1 Tank Company, including;

- 1x Team Yankee Complete Rules A5 Mini Version,

- 3x Plastic M1 or IPM1 tanks,

- 2x Plastic Cobra helicopters,

- 2x Decal Sheets, and

- 6x Unit Cards.

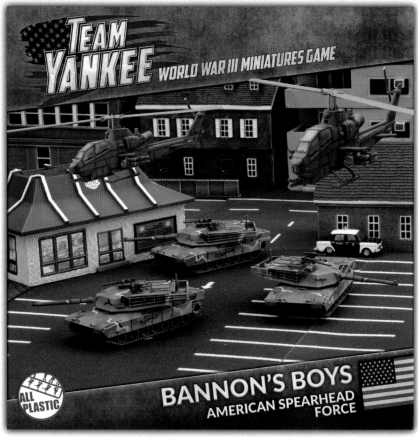

TUSABX3
RYAN'S LEATHERNECKS

Ryan's Leathernecks contains all the American models you need to begin building a Marine M60 Tank Company, including;

- 1x Team Yankee Complete Rules A5 Mini Version,

- 3x Plastic M60 tanks,

- 6x Plastic HMMWVs,

- 1x Decal Sheet, and

- 6x Unit Cards.

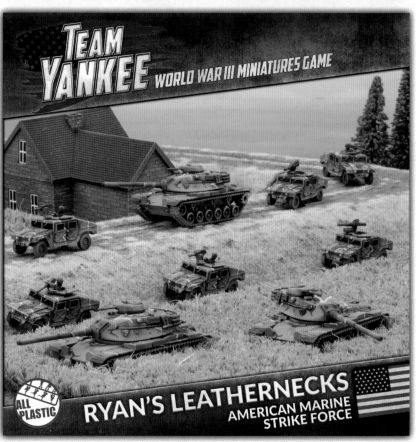

For the complete range of tokens, templates and other gaming accessories, visit your local stockist or www.Team-Yankee.com

Also available is the complete range of pre-painted 'Battlefield In A Box' terrain, as seen throughout this book.

TUBX08

CONTAINS:
5x Plastic IPM1 or M1 Abrams Tanks
1x Plastic Tank Commander Sprue
1x Decal Sheet
5x Unit Cards

M1 Abrams

IPM1 Abrams

Abrams Tank Platoon (Plastic)

TUBX11

CONTAINS:
5x Plastic M60 Patton Tanks
1x Plastic Tank Commander Sprue
1x Decal Sheet
8x Unit Cards

M60 Patton Tank Platoon (Plastic)

TUBX16

CONTAINS:
5x Plastic LAV Vehicles
2x Plastic AT Upgrades
1x Plastic Tank Commander Sprue
1x Mortar Crew Sprue
1x Decal Sheet
6x Unit Cards

LAV-AT

LAV-M

LAV-25

LAV Platoon (Plastic)

TUBX05

x2

CONTAINS:
2x Plastic AH-1 Cobra Attack Helicopters
2x Plastic Flight Stands
8x Rare-earth Magnets
2x Decal Sheets
1x Unit Card

Cobra Attack Helicopter Platoon (Plastic)

TUBX07

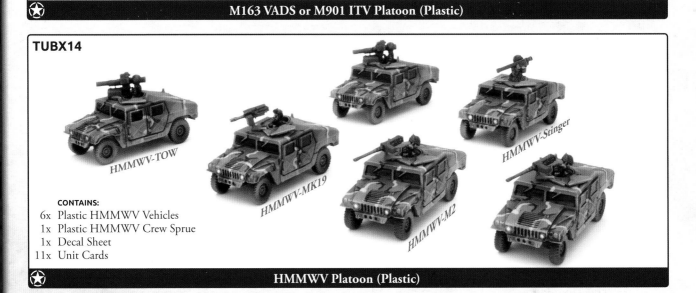

x2

CONTAINS:
2x Plastic UH-1 Huey Transport Helicopters
2x Plastic Flight Stands
8x Rare-earth Magnets
1x Decal Sheet
2x Unit Cards

Contains options to build as Marine Hueys.

UH-1 Huey Helicopter Platoon (Plastic)

TUBX02

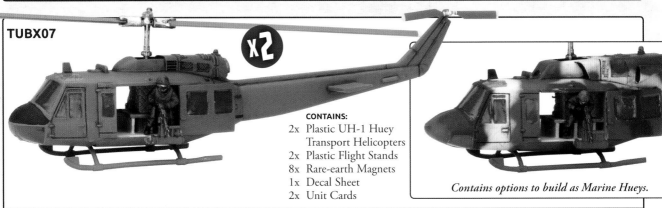

M901 ITV

M163 VADS

CONTAINS:
4x Plastic M163 VADS or M901 ITV Vehicles
1x Decal Sheet
5x Unit Cards

M163 VADS or M901 ITV Platoon (Plastic)

TUBX14

HMMWV-TOW

HMMWV-MK19

HMMWV-M2

HMMWV-Stinger

CONTAINS:
6x Plastic HMMWV Vehicles
1x Plastic HMMWV Crew Sprue
1x Decal Sheet
11x Unit Cards

HMMWV Platoon (Plastic)

TUBX03

M113 APC

M106 Mortar

CONTAINS:
4x Plastic M113 APCs or
    M106 Mortars
4x M113 Commander and Dragon Sprues
2x M106 Mortar Crew Sprues
1x Decal Sheet
7x Unit Cards

M113 Platoon (Plastic)

TUBX13

*This box can make either a
UH-1 Huey Rifle Platoon,
or a Marine Rifle Platoon*

M249 SAW teams

M47 Dragon
missile teams

M60 GPMG teams

SMAW teams

60mm mortar team

M16 Rifle team

CONTAINS:
1x M16 Rifle team
9x M249 SAW teams
    with M72 LAW anti-tank
2x M47 Dragon missile teams
2x M60 GPMG teams
2x SMAW teams
1x M224 60mm mortar team
7x Unit Cards

Rifle Platoon

TUS702

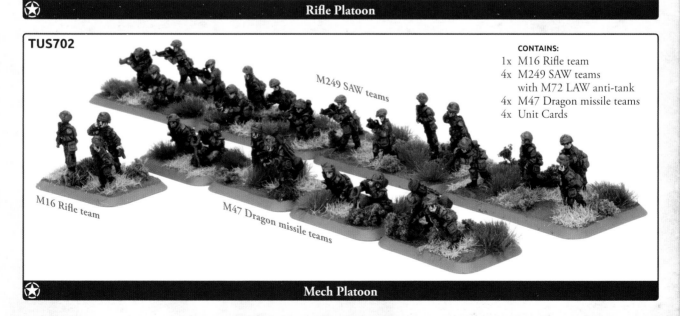

M249 SAW teams

CONTAINS:
1x M16 Rifle team
4x M249 SAW teams
    with M72 LAW anti-tank
4x M47 Dragon missile teams
4x Unit Cards

M16 Rifle team

M47 Dragon missile teams

Mech Platoon

TUBX17

CONTAINS:

5x M551 Sheridan Tank
1x Plastic Tank Commander Sprue
1x Decal Sheet
1x Unit Card

M551 Sheridan Tank Platoon

TUBX09

CONTAINS:

4x M48 Chaparral SAM Launchers
1x Decal Sheet
1x Unit Card

M48 Chaparral SAM Platoon

TUBX10

CONTAINS:

4x M247 Sergeant York AA Vehicles
1x Decal Sheet
1x Unit Card

M247 Sergeant York AA Platoon

TUBX06

CONTAINS:
- 2x A-10 Warthog Aircraft
- 2x Plastic Flight Stands
- 4x Rare-earth Magnets
- 1x Decal Sheet
- 1x Unit Card

x2

A-10 Warthog Fighter Flight

TUBX12

CONTAINS:
- 2x AV-8 Harrier Aircraft
- 2x Plastic Flight Stands
- 4x Rare-earth Magnets
- 1x Decal Sheet
- 1x Unit Card

x2

AV-8 Harrier Attack Flight

TUBX15

CONTAINS:
- 2x AAVP7 Armored Personnel Carriers
- 1x Plastic Tank Commander Sprue
- 1x Decal Sheet
- 1x Unit Card

AAVP7 Platoon

TUBX04

CONTAINS:
- 3x M109 155mm Self-propelled Howitzers
- 1x Minefield Token
- 2x Unit Cards

M109 Field Artillery Battery

M60 PATTON

M60A1 & M60A3

Crew: 4 - commander, gunner, loader, driver
Weight: 52.6 tonnes
Length: 9.309m (30' 6.5")
Width: 3.63m (11' 11")
Height: 3.213m (10' 6.5")
Weapons: M68 105mm gun
M85 .50 cal MG
M73 7.62mm MG
Armour: Upper Glacis 109mm (4.29") at 65°
Turret Front 250mm (10") equivalent
Speed: 72 km/h (45 mph)
Engine: Continental AVDS-1790-2 V12, air-cooled
Twin-turbo diesal engine
560 kW (750 hp)
Range: 480 km (300 miles)

The M60 Patton tank entered service with the US Army in 1960. It was the first US tank to be designated a Main Battle Tank, incorporating the speed and mobility of a medium tank with the armour and firepower of a heavy tank. During its long career it underwent several upgrades, including the unsuccessful M60A2 missile tank. The M60 also served with the US Marine Corps from 1973.

· The M60A1 Patton as used by the US Marine corps uses the AOS stabilisation kit, while the M60A3 as used by the Army has a new stabilisation system linked to the ballistics computer.

· The M60A3 added a thermal sleeve to the gun barrel to reduce gun droop under sustained fire.

· The M60A1 had Infrared (IR) night fighting equipment, while the M60A3 has more advanced Thermal Imaging (TI).

M60A1 Patton

M60A3 Patton

6' / 1.8m

The M60 tank started life as an upgrade to the M48 Patton to increase its operational range and mobility with minimal refuelling and servicing. It also included an improved main armament. By 1958, a new tank incorporating these features began testing as the XM60.

The new main gun was a hybrid of the British 105mm L7A1 barrel (as found in the West German Leopard 1 among others) and the US developed T254E2 breech and was designated the M68.

The XM60 was officially adopted into service with the US Army in 1960. Initially, the M60 used a modified M48 turret fitted with the new M68 105mm gun, but in 1962 a new turret was introduced as the M60A1. The new turret was larger, with an improved ballistic shape. The M60A1 also made improvements to armour, suspension, and drive train. Combination day and infrared (IR) periscopes were introduced for the gunner and the commander.

The M60A1 remained in production from 1962 until 1980. Numerous improvements were made to the M60A1 during its production. In 1972 Add-On Stabilization (AOS) kits were added to M60A1 tanks' existing hydraulic gun control systems. At short to medium ranges, a moving M60A1 (AOS) hit more than 50% of the time in testing, while hits without a stabilizer were essentially zero.

In 1975, a new engine with improved service life and reliability was fitted. Passive night vision sights for the gunner and commander and a new night vision device for the driver were added in 1977.

In 1978, the M60A3 went into production. It included new technology, such as smoke dischargers, a laser rangefinder that could be used by both commander and gunner, an M21 ballistic computer, a new turret stabilization system, and a Tank Thermal Sight (TTS). This system proved even better than that fitted to the M1 Abrams.